Points of Grace
Empowerment for Hard Times

Stuart Cedrone, Ph.D.

TEACH Services, Inc.
PUBLISHING
www.TEACHServices.com • (800) 367-1844

World rights reserved. This book or any portion thereof may not be copied or reproduced in any form or manner whatever, except as provided by law, without the written permission of the publisher, except by a reviewer who may quote brief passages in a review.

The author assumes full responsibility for the accuracy of all facts and quotations as cited in this book. The opinions expressed in this book are the author's personal views and interpretations, and do not necessarily reflect those of the publisher.

This book is provided with the understanding that the publisher is not engaged in giving spiritual, legal, medical, or other professional advice. If authoritative advice is needed, the reader should seek the counsel of a competent professional.

Copyright © 2020 Stuart Cedrone
Copyright © 2020 TEACH Services, Inc.
ISBN-13: 978-1-4796-1187-4 (Paperback)
ISBN-13: 978-1-4796-1188-1 (ePub)
Library of Congress Control Number: 2020908402

Unless otherwise indicated, all Scripture quotations are from The Holy Bible New International Version®. (NIV). Copyright © 1973, 1978, 1984 by International Bible Society. All rights reserved. Other scriptures are taken from The King James Version; The Holy Bible, New King James Version® (NKJV), copyright © 1979, 1980, 1982, HarperCollins. Used by permission of Thomas Nelson Publishers; Revised Standard Version of the Bible (RSV), *© 1952 [2nd edition, 1971] by the Division of Christian Education of the National Council of the Churches of Christ in the United States of America. Used by permission. All rights reserved.*

www.TEACHServices.com • (800) 367-1844

Dedication

This book is dedicated to Richard D'Avanzo, PhD, mentor, friend, and brother in Christ.

Every believer in Christ looks only to our Savior for salvation and ultimate comfort—this is a given. Nevertheless, it's nice to know a person who lives wholeheartedly for Jesus in the manner that Richard did. One can safely look to such a person for wise counsel during times of extremity, as I and many others often did.

Richard endured many difficult years of pain and hardship, and he remained faithful to Jesus Christ through every one of these years. He grew to know his Savior quite intimately as a true Friend through these seasons of adversity, and Jesus always delivered him.

Ultimately, He brought him forth as gold.

Richard trusted every aspect of his life to Jesus, and he truly loved Him. He sought to inspire others to likewise trust and love Him and to serve Him with all their hearts.

Those of us who knew Richard seek to preserve his legacy by being faithful servants to Christ in every area of our lives—just as he was.

I hope God has led someone like Richard into your life. I am so thankful to have had him in mine.

Praise the Lord.

Table of Contents

Dedication iii

Introduction 7

1. Crises and Brokenness 9

2. God Punished Christ 16

3. God Tested Christ 22

4. We Are Accepted in Christ 32

5. We Never Get Past Acceptance in Christ 41

6. We Have Obeyed God's Commandments in Christ, Part 1 52

7. We Have Obeyed God's Commandments in Christ, Part 2 60

8. We Are Growing in Christ, Part 1 71

9. We Are Growing in Christ, Part 2 80

10. We Are Born Again in Christ 87

11. Our Sinful Body Is Dead in Christ 95

12. We are Perfectly Surrendered in Christ 101

13 We Are Secure in Christ 106

14. We Are Reconciled to Our Past in Christ 111

15. We Have a New Beginning (Always) in Christ 116

16. Concluding Thoughts 122

Introduction

    I have experienced many brutal trials and heart-wrenching failures in my life. Most people have. I have learned, however, that these painful experiences of adversity and defeat can cause us to cry out to God in authentic ways of which we are incapable at other times—and this is the key to our growth.
    Why are we incapable of crying out to God in authentic ways except during times of extremity? It is simply because, at other times, we are trying desperately to remain *in control*. Ever since Adam and Eve took matters into their own hands in the Garden of Eden, the exercise of control has come quite naturally to us. We manipulate matters to insulate ourselves from shame and vulnerability, and we don't even realize we're doing it.
    Seemingly hopeless situations, however, have a way of changing this. These bruising ordeals drive most of us to cry out in anguish to a power greater than ourselves, and this, of course, is a form of *relinquishing* control. Times of adversity thus have the potential to break the projection and denial that have been woven into the fabric of our being since the Fall. They become the gateway to honesty and truth.
    I will develop this theme in the pages that follow in order to help us to properly understand the times of hopelessness that God allows in our lives. I will also illuminate various points of grace that provide insight and inspire courage. These points of grace are vitally important to ensure that we do not misinterpret the merciful activity of God during these critical

times. By the conclusion of this study, I hope each of us will see clearly that the primary purpose of trials is to bring each of us to a state of brokenness. This humbling of our willful pride allows each of us to do what is completely *un*natural for us to do since the Fall, namely, to *confess the truth*.

As you read the chapters of this book, I hope you will remember that God's posture toward you is always one of tenderness and compassion. This is true in good times as well as in terrible times. It doesn't matter if you are joyfully basking in the sunshine on the mountaintop or painfully navigating through the deepest and darkest part of the valley. God *always* has caring thoughts and sympathetic feelings toward you, for anything opposed to this disposition is "strange" and "alien" to His tender and merciful heart (Isaiah 28:21; 1 John 4:8).

God *loves* you!

Chapter 1
Crises and Brokenness

*"Do not be deceived: God cannot be mocked.
A man reaps what he sows."*

(Galatians 6:7)

Life has a way of catching up with us, doesn't it? Any insensitivity on our part, however expressed, has a way of finding a path back to us through the words and actions of others. And when it finds its way back to us, it has a way of breaking us.

I remember the first time I was broken. I had just completed a doctoral program in philosophy at the University of Connecticut, and I had become very proud of my abilities. I had also become quite dogmatic and close-minded. I had it all figured out.

I knew nothing of my personal pride and arrogance at this time because God had not yet allowed me to "bottom out." This process began quickly after my graduation, however, because the path I had chosen ran its course to completion. I found myself facing an employment situation where there were hundreds of applicants for each of the few academic positions that were advertised, and I also found myself facing a "motivational" situation where the mere thought of continuing to teach philosophy was like death to me.

So, I was dying.

I was in a suicidal state for about two years, and, during this time, God allowed me to witness much of my hardness and dogmatism as these qualities found their way back to me through the words and actions of others. Truly, what goes around comes around—"As you have done, it will be done to you; your deeds will return upon your own head" (Obadiah 15). And again: "With the measure you use, it will be measured to you" (Matthew 7:2). Consider the comments of a Christian author in relation to the above verses:

> Whatever we give, we shall receive again . . . evil imparted . . . returns again. Everyone who has been free to condemn or discourage, will in his own experience be brought over the [same] ground where he has caused others to pass; he will feel what they have suffered because of his want of sympathy and tenderness.
>
> It is the love of God toward us that has decreed this. He would lead us to abhor our own hardness of heart and to open our hearts to let Jesus abide in them. And thus, out of evil, good is brought, and what appeared a curse becomes a blessing.[1]

Truly, it is the love of God—not the punishment of God—that decrees these difficult times in our lives when our arrogance and insensitivity find their way back to us, and God's love is working during these times so that the appointed crisis may be—not a curse—but, rather, a blessing.

During my many personal crises, I have always experienced the tender influence of the Holy Spirit as He brought comfort and acceptance to me. This was especially true during the painful times when I was facing condemning and judgmental spirits in the people around me. The Holy Spirit caused me to remember the many times I had caused similar pain and discouragement to others. He thus used these experiences to awaken me to my great need of sensitivity and compassion, and He prompted me to cry out to my Father in Christ for courage and strength.

Also, because the pain I experienced during these crises was raw and intense (as it is during *all* crises), the awareness of my lack of sympathy toward others was likewise raw and intense, so it went deep—to my core. I was thus brought to the point where I could acknowledge the hardness of my heart in ways I formerly never could, and this acknowl-

---

[1] Ellen White, *Thoughts from the Mount of Blessing* (https://1ref.us/zc, accessed February 10, 2020), p. 136.

edgement and subsequent confession led to long-needed growth. Truly, God works *all* things together for good in the lives of those who love Him (Romans 8:28).

One point of grace I learned during my initial extremity (and during others as well) is this:

I never grow except during a crisis.

This is so because, during times of non-crisis, I am in "cruise control." That is, I am "cruising" along in my insensitivity and dogmatism by the power of a prideful (and unrecognized) inertia that carries me forward. This "cruise control" is in full operation even if the prideful inertia is expressed only in passive ways that seem quite harmless.

I have no doubt that all of us are in the grip of this inertia until God intervenes. We are stubborn in ways we do not realize, and if this stubbornness is not broken, we remain bound by the inertia of our self-will. "I have seen these people," the Lord said to Moses, "and they are a stiff-necked people" (Exodus 32:9). This statement about the Israelites is no less true of us than it was of them. We have stiff necks that must be broken, and the only way to break them is through the hard, crunching trials that God ordains in tender and merciful ways.

> *We are stubborn in ways we do not realize, and if this stubbornness is not broken, we remain bound by the inertia of our self-will.*

The apostle Peter writes that we should not be surprised by this activity of our heavenly Father. He even states that we should rejoice in it: "Beloved, do not think it strange concerning the fiery trial which is to try you, as though some strange thing happened to you; but rejoice to the extent that you partake of Christ's sufferings, that when His glory is revealed, you may also be glad with exceeding joy" (1 Peter 4:12, 13, NKJV).

A further point of grace I have learned during my many trials is this: Not only do I never grow without a crisis, but I also never grow unless the crisis in which I find myself is so severe that the pieces of my shattered life seem as if they will never fit back together. In other words, I never grow unless the fiery ordeal I am experiencing is so severe that my situation seems *hopeless*.

And why do I never grow unless my situation seems hopeless? It is because it is only during times of hopelessness that I feel completely and utterly *helpless*. And it is only when I feel completely and utterly helpless that I am brought to the point of relinquishing the control of my life—a control that, under normal circumstances, I hold onto *at any cost*. In short, it is only during times of hopelessness that I am brought to the place that I can be *broken*.

What do I mean by being broken? Simply this:

I mean to be humbled to the point that I am delivered from the natural "stiff-necked" tendency to live a life of proud autonomy that is independent of my Creator's will.

To accomplish this deliverance, God allows all of us to reach the end of our ropes (the *absolute* end—where there is no rope left to tie a knot and hold on). God allows us to reach this place in the hope that proud, arrogant creatures like you and me will finally admit, "You know, I think my Creator knows best." It is at this point that we stop trying to go it alone and start seeking His will for our lives.

Let's face an obvious truth here: As rational creatures of our God and Creator, we are acting in a manner that makes sense *only* when we are acting in harmony with His will for our lives. Since God obviously wants us to live purposeful lives that make sense, He is *always* working to bring us to a place where we cease living autonomous lives of irrational independence. He brings us to the point where we see that our proud desire to always be the one in control, to always be the one calling the shots is what brings us to crisis points of desperation. We thus realize that "going with the flow" of our natural, manipulative drive to be independent of God just *does not work*. (I remember a song that was popular many years ago that expresses this thought. It was "Everybody Wants to Rule the World.")

We see this desire for autonomy and independence expressed in the lives of Adam and Eve in the Garden of Eden. Eve believes the lie of the serpent that she will be "like God," so she eats the forbidden fruit of the tree of the knowledge of good and evil (Genesis 3:1–6). Adam, though not deceived (2 Timothy 2:14), eats the fruit as well (Genesis 3:6)—apparently because he cannot bear the thought of life without Eve. By these acts of rebellion, Adam and Eve clearly attempt to escape their dependency upon the Creator and endeavor to be autonomous. That is, they try to live lives that are independent from God's will, and this leaves them feeling fearful, ashamed, and seemingly incapable of acknowledging and confessing the truth of what they have done.

They are initially conscience-stricken because of their nakedness, so they sew fig leaves for coverings (Genesis 3:7). Then they run and hide from the presence of God when they hear Him in the garden (Genesis 3:8). When God calls to Adam, he replies that he is afraid and is hiding because he is naked (Genesis 3:10). God asks, "Who told you that you were naked? Have you eaten from the tree that I commanded you not to eat from?" (Genesis 3:11)

Adam does not confess that he has done this; rather, he "explains" (and, thus, in his own mind, justifies) his action by blaming Eve—"the woman you put here with me—she gave me some fruit from the tree, and I ate it" (Genesis 3:12). When God questions Eve, she also does not confess that she has done wrong. Like Adam, she "explains" (and thus justifies) her actions by blaming the serpent (the creature You allowed to be in the garden "deceived me"—Genesis 3:13).

Clearly, Adam and Eve's acts of rebellion have resulted in their being thoroughly immersed in denial, for they are incapable of honestly confessing the truth of their wrongdoing. In their minds, God Himself, as the ultimate first cause, has become the convenient source of the problem. God has also become more of an enemy than a friend, for He is now someone from whom the Eden pair feel they must hide. (*Hide* from their *Creator?!* This is our inherited inclination as well.)

God pronounces judgment by informing them that there will be difficult times ahead. Eve's childbearing pains will be "very severe" (Genesis 3:16), and Adam's work will involve "painful toil" on an earth that will now produce "thorns and thistles" (Genesis 3:17, 18). God also informs Adam that he is not, in fact, an independent being that possesses true autonomy. He tells him, "Dust you are and to dust you will return" (Genesis 3:19).

We learn from this biblical narrative of the Fall that there are legitimate reasons God allows times of extremity in our lives. The first reason is one I have already mentioned, namely,

- *To break us of our inherent tendency to live lives of irrational independence and autonomy.*

We see two *additional* reasons for the "fiery ordeals" that God allows in our lives because of tendencies that surfaced in Adam and Eve after the Fall:

- *To break the tendency to offer self-justifying excuses instead of honestly confessing the truth.*
- *To break the tendency to fear God and thus regard Him as someone from whom we must hide.*

"Fiery ordeals" are thus needed for these three important reasons. How else can the truth of God's Word enter our hardened hearts but through times of extremity that bring brokenness and contrition?

The points of grace that I cover in this book will help us to see the crises in our lives as the blessings God intends them to be. They will also help us to find strength in Christ to face trying circumstances with grace and courage. I will often share how a point of grace has helped me during a time of personal crisis, but even if I do not share such a personal application, each point of grace, when applied, will provide needed strength and insight to persevere through difficult times.

In closing, let us remember the words of Andrew Murray whenever we are going through times of crisis and extremity. In 1895 he was suffering terribly from back pain, and, as he was eating breakfast in his room, his hostess told him of a woman downstairs who was in great trouble and wanted to know if he had any advice for her. Murray handed the hostess a piece of paper on which he had been writing. He said, "Give her this advice I'm writing down for myself. It may be that she'll find it helpful."

This is what was written:

"In time of trouble, say, 'First, He brought me here. It is by His will I am in this strait place; in that I will rest.'

"Next, 'He will keep me here in His love, and give me grace in this trial to behave as His child.'

"Then say, 'He will make the trial a blessing, teaching me lessons He intends me to learn, and working in me the grace He means to bestow.'

"And last, say, 'In His good time He can bring me out again. How and when, He knows.'

"Therefore, say 'I am here (1) by God's appointment, (2) in His keeping, (3) under His training, (4) for His time.'"[2]

These words should encourage all of us, for, truly, God never intends to "park" us in a valley to die of brokenness and despair. Rather, He promises to walk us *through* the valley (Psalm 23:4) to the other side. He

---

2 Andrew Murray, quoted by Ray C. Stedman, in "How to Kill a Lion on a Snowy Day," Nov. 4, 1973, available at https://1ref.us/zd, accessed February 10, 2020.

will surely do this for all of us—in *His* time. We will then feel, once again, the intense warmth and comfort of His acceptance and love, even though God was there for us all the time.

* * *

Praise God from whom all blessings flow.[3]

---

[3] Written in 1674 by Thomas Ken as the first line in the final stanza of two hymns, *Awake, My Soul, and with the Sun* and *Glory to Thee, My God, This Night*, in what is known as "The Doxology."

Chapter 2
God Punished Christ

> *But he was pierced for our transgressions,*
> *He was crushed for our iniquities;*
> *The punishment that brought us peace was on him,*
> *And by his wounds we are healed.*
>
> (Isaiah 53:5)

The first point of grace we must learn when going through hard times is this: God punished Christ for everything we did to bring the crisis upon us, so there is no punishment left for us.

This is an area in which I struggled mightily when I was "bottoming out" after completing my doctoral degree. I understood (on a "theoretical" level) that God had punished Christ for my many sins, but I was braced to resist the application of this truth to me personally because I was painfully aware that I had brought the crisis upon myself through my arrogance and pride. I knew that *I myself* deserved punishment for my abominable behavior, so I felt incapable of accepting the fact that God had punished *another* in my behalf.

It just seemed wrong.

Despite this painful awareness that I was the one who deserved punishment, God eventually brought me to the point where I realized I would never be delivered from my extremity until I claimed by faith the truth that He laid all the punishment I deserved upon Jesus. And why would I not be delivered until I claimed this truth by faith? Because the wages of sin is death (Romans 6:23), and I had sinned (Romans 3:23). Therefore, I deserved—not deliverance—but, rather, *death*. I thus needed to claim by faith the truth that God laid all the punishment I deserved upon Jesus. Only in this way would the "wages of sin" be paid in my behalf; therefore, only in this way could I claim—in *Jesus'* name—God's many promises of deliverance

During crises in our lives, we often find it difficult to hold fast to this promise that God laid the punishment we deserve upon Jesus because crises are times when we will feel least worthy to claim anything. Reflect again upon the Scripture quoted at the beginning of this chapter: "But he was pierced for our transgressions, he was crushed for our iniquities; the punishment that brought us peace was on him, and by his wounds we are healed" (Isaiah 53:5). We doubtless know this text of Scripture, just as we know many other texts of Scripture that state that God punished Jesus for our sins. But we are prone to doubt the truth of these statements because we feel uncomfortable saying something like, "God punished Jesus for my abominable behavior." We might even think there is some sort of Christian virtue in standing up like a real man (or a real woman) and graciously accepting a just penalty from the Almighty. I hope we eventually come to realize, however, that there is never any virtue in such a posture toward our merciful heavenly Father, for He has no punishment left to dole out to us. Truly, it was all laid upon our Savior.

In our fallen state, we are naturally prone to seek the autonomy and independence that Adam and Eve sought in the Garden of Eden; therefore, we have a difficult time accepting that the punishment we deserve was laid upon Christ. We are driven by a deep desire to be *in control*—even of our own salvation. So, God will continue to allow us to experience the pain and heartache of our autonomous ways until we are humbled by His grace. He will continue to usher us into the "fiery ordeals" of which Peter speaks until we are broken of this deep desire to exercise control over our lives and the lives of others. God desires that we begin to appreciate Him with a heart softened by His mercy and love rather than with one hardened by legalistic manipulation and works.

Notice that the Bible states, not only that God punished Christ for our sin but also that "it *pleased* the Lord to bruise Him (emphasis added)" (Isaiah 53:10, NKJV).

Can we even *begin* to comprehend such love and mercy for us?

I have no doubt that it is impossible for us to fully appreciate such boundless love, but I hope we can at least understand that, if it pleased God to bruise Jesus in our behalf, it certainly does *not* please Him if we refuse to accept this gift of grace to us. And we are surely refusing this merciful gift of grace when we adopt a posture of thinking that we must accept punishment from our heavenly Father.

By thinking that we must accept punishment from God, we are effectively asserting (in a passively proud sort of way) that the punishment He has already laid upon His Son is somehow insufficient (or, worse yet, not needed or desired) in our cases. May God help each of us to understand that there is never any virtue in attempting to graciously accept punishment from Him. Such a posture reveals a state of deep delusion, for it completely distorts His character as well as the nature of His plan for our salvation.

> *By thinking that we must accept punishment from God, we are effectively asserting (in a passively proud sort of way) that the punishment He has already laid upon His Son is somehow insufficient (or, worse yet, not needed or desired) in our cases.*

Surely those of us who have been born into God's family experience the compassionate care of the divine nature. Do you not experience the tender mercies of God during times of sweet communion with Him? We should thus know through firsthand experience that our heavenly Father would never seek to punish us in the ways that we, as fallen sinners, seek to punish others who cross our wills.

Also, the Bible states plainly that, for God, vengeance is a "strange work" (Isaiah 28:21). It also states that He takes "no pleasure in the death of the wicked" (Ezekiel 33:11). Indeed, the Bible makes it clear that our heavenly Father will gladly take all punishment upon Himself and freely justify anyone who simply humbles himself by confessing the truth of his lost condition (Luke 18:13, 14).

The unfortunate reality, however, is that most people will not humble themselves in this way because most are determined to be proud and autonomous—even if this means that they must be dishonest and deceitful. In short, most are People of the Lie[4] (John 8:43–45) rather than People of the Truth (John 18:37).

To summarize, when we encounter difficult times, we often have a piercing awareness that we deserve punishment. This is quite natural, and the feeling is hard to shake because we have a deep sense that we have brought the extremity upon ourselves. We thus believe we must be punished for our waywardness. This sense of deserving punishment reflects the truth of our situation, for we know that justice demands a price to be paid for the hardness of heart that was committed by miserable wretches like us. What we must realize in the face of this truth is that Jesus *became* the miserable wretch who was punished in our behalf. This is what He was in God's eyes when He hung upon the cross.

Amazing love!

We should not minimize this truth because we know in our hearts that we ourselves are the true wretches. We should not allow ourselves to wallow around and say things like, "I'm such a bad person. I deserve bad things in my life. I brought all of this upon myself. I will take God's punishment like a real man (or a real woman)." Clearly, such a posture effectively denies the truth that Jesus became the punished wretch in our behalf.

When we finally allow ourselves to accept redemption in Christ as we should, we realize that thoughts of "graciously" accepting punishment from God are expressions of rebellion and unbelief. They represent nothing less than adamant refusals to be grounded in God's grace, and only a grounding in God's grace allows the door of deliverance to be opened for us. Once again, this is true because only a grounding in grace places us in a position where we may justifiably claim, in Jesus' name, God's many promises of deliverance.

Personally, I have found that most of us are willing to accept the truth of God's grace only if it does not come too close to home. That is, we will accept the truth that Jesus died for our sins in an abstract, theological way, but if this truth should ever get too close, too personal—then we balk. We respond in this way because proud, autonomous creatures like you and me

---

4   This is a phrase employed by M. Scott Peck, *People of the Lie: The Hope for Healing Human Evil* (New York, NY: Simon & Schuster, 1983).

are uncomfortable accepting the truth of our "creaturehood." We would rather retain the control of our lives and go it alone than relinquish this control, cry out to God, and place the total weight of our desperate need upon *Him*. We are far more comfortable moaning and groaning and griping and complaining about anything and everything that is wrong in our lives. All of our elaborate excuses, our many gripes and complaints—these have become like a nice, soft easy chair or a "company of sympathizing friends," and we have become accustomed to settling into them.[5] They are comfortable, and they keep us protected. Most of all, they allow us to continue in our stubborn ways without having to be broken—of our pride, our self-will, and our hardness of heart.

But there is no way around being broken, for only in this way are we delivered from the projection and denial that come so naturally to us in our fallen state. Only in this way are we brought to a place where we begin to acknowledge *truth*—about our situation, about God, and about ourselves.

To give a practical application of this principle, think of the experiences of Judas and Peter. Each betrayed the trust of Christ (although, admittedly, in different ways). Judas was unwilling to be broken of his pride and self-will. He refused to relinquish the control of his life, even though Christ treated him with the utmost understanding and mercy throughout the course of his betrayal. Jesus even washed Judas' feet along with the other disciples. All of this was to no avail, however, as Judas was determined to persist in his proud path of unbrokenness. He thus rendered himself incapable of repentance and finally "went and hanged himself" (Matthew 27:5).

Peter, on the other hand, met a different fate. Imagine him as he begins to "curse and swear" and eventually yell, "I do not know the Man!" (Matthew 26:74, NKJV) Clearly, this is a person who is feeling only shame because of his association with Jesus. (I hope all of us will allow ourselves to confess the times when *we* have felt such shame of our Savior.) At the precise time when Peter is feeling this shame, the Bible states, "... the rooster crowed. The Lord turned and looked straight at Peter. Then Peter remembered the word the Lord had spoken to him: 'Before the rooster crows today, you will disown me three times.' And he went outside and wept bitterly" (Luke 22:60–62).

---

[5] Hannah Whitall Smith, *The Christian's Secret of a Happy Life* (Chicago: Fleming H. Revell Company, 1888, 1916), p. 109, available at https://1ref.us/ze, accessed February 10, 2020.

Imagine getting a tender look from Jesus just as you finish denying Him for the third time! Unlike Judas, however, Peter was humbled (to the *dust!*) by this expression of mercy from his Savior. He was broken of his pride and self-will, so he responded by weeping in repentance rather than hanging himself. The result of this experience is that the Bible records Peter issuing the following words to the Jews in Jerusalem shortly after Christ's ascension: "You denied the Holy One and the Just" (Acts 3:14).

Do you see how quickly God can restore a person? Peter uttered these words shortly after Pentecost, so it was probably about eight weeks after his own personal denial of Christ. Yet Peter is not whining and moaning. He is not thinking of hanging himself because of overwhelming regret and remorse. Rather, he is boldly bearing witness to the Jews' denial of Jesus—even though he himself openly denied his Savior and Lord just two months prior.

Truly, God works *all* things together for good in the lives of those who love Him (Romans 8:28), and in precisely those areas in which we are weak, He makes us *strong*. It should therefore come as no surprise that He chose Peter to give this forceful message to the Jews in Jerusalem.

In conclusion: There is no punitive element to any trial God allows, for God has taken all the punishment upon Himself in the person of Jesus, our Savior. And, miracle of miracles, it *pleased* the Father to do this for us.

"Christ was treated as we deserve, that we might be treated as He deserves."[6]

* * *

Praise God from whom all blessings flow.

---

[6] Ellen White, *Desire of Ages* (https://1ref.us/zf, accessed February 10, 2020), p. 25.

Chapter 3
God Tested Christ

> *Then Jesus was led by the Spirit into the wilderness*
> *To be tempted by the devil.*
>
> *(Matthew 4:1)*

We learned in the previous chapter that there is no punitive element to any trial in our lives because God laid all the punishment for our sins upon Jesus. In the present chapter I will show that there is likewise no "works" element to any trial because the Father is fully satisfied that His Son passed every test in our behalf.

The central point here is that Jesus is primarily our *Savior*, not our example[7] (Matthew 1:21). Thus, His life of unbroken obedience is primarily a *gift* for us to receive rather than a *standard* for us to attain. When this truth enters our hearts by faith, we have peace with God, freedom in Christ—and rest. If this truth does not enter our hearts by faith, then we have no peace with God, no freedom in Christ—and no rest. On the contrary, we live lives filled with continual unsettledness as we strive to attain the standard of a perfect example. Surely, this is no way to live for believers who claim to be saved by grace.

---

[7] Christ is, of course, our example. (I take this to be obvious.) Nevertheless, Christ is not *primarily* our example, and His role as our example has nothing to do with the *root* of our salvation.

Personally, I have found that engaging in some "gut it out" mode during difficult times in my life accomplishes nothing. I have also found that there is no virtue in this approach. This is so because—as with punishment—believing that God is trying to extract some "works" element from us during the trials of our lives completely distorts His character and His purpose.

Since God is an omniscient being, He obviously knows all of us completely; therefore, He has no need to "test" us by hard times to determine the content of our hearts. He knows what we can bear and when we will crumble. He has no need for us to perform some work to prove something to Him.

Remember, the perfect life needed for salvation has already been accomplished *for us* in the person of Jesus, and God's word is clear that this perfect life is given to the believer as a *gift* (Romans 6:23). Everything in relation to the perfect standard needed for salvation is therefore a *settled matter* with God.

I remember when I was trying to "prove" myself by working out of the pit I was in when I hit bottom. The more I tried, the more I became entrenched in a sinful mode of behavior that battered my already-tortured conscience. I was completely enslaved by sins of indulgence during this time, and I seemed incapable of being motivated to work for God and His kingdom. I desired only to do things like watch movies, stuff myself with food and lie in bed feeling sorry for myself.

I realize that people descend into much darker pits of sin than this, and I do not mean to make light of their reality by simply mentioning areas like watching movies or overeating. I have certainly struggled in other areas of my life during later years. I remember starting to smoke again (something I had left behind when I initially became a Christian), and I also remember having to install an Internet filter on my computer at one time to block sites related to online pornography.

> *It was only as I ceased self-conscious efforts to prove myself and instead rested in the finished work of Jesus, my Savior, that beneficial fruit began to flow from my life.*

Returning to my efforts to "prove" myself, I will state this: As long as I continued in this mode, just so long did I continue to be overwhelmed with my inadequacy. It was only as I *ceased* self-conscious efforts to prove myself and instead *rested* in the finished work of Jesus, my Savior, that beneficial fruit began to flow from my life.

Truly, God does not desire that crisis situations be times when we perform heroic tasks for Him. He has promised to do the progressive work necessary for our sanctification, and there is plenty of time for Him to accomplish this work on the other side of the crisis when we are better grounded in His grace. But *during* a crisis, He desires that we simply *rest* in the perfect work that Christ has already accomplished *for us*.

It is this rest and cessation from works that allow us to see

- Truth about our situation
- Truth about God
- Truth about the condition of our hearts

Remember, our natural condition since the Fall is one of projection and denial. It therefore comes *naturally* to us to be autonomous and independent, to blame others and God for our problems, and to be completely blind to the truth. We are so blind to the truth that our natural response to our merciful Creator and Redeemer is to think of Him as someone from whom we must run and hide!

Our Father in heaven uses difficult times to break these tendencies in us so that we can reach a position where we are able to receive the truth. If we adopt a works-oriented posture where we believe we must "gut it out," then we will thwart this grace-centered work that He seeks to accomplish for us. We will be so absorbed with our efforts to bear up under a crushing load that we will be incapable of seeing anything God is trying to reveal to us.

We will be thinking thoughts like,

- *I need to be strong.*
- *I need to make it through this.*
- *I can't break down.*

I would venture to say that the thought, *I can't break down*, is one that most of us think repeatedly during difficult times. I repeated these words to myself quite often when I was persevering through the two years that I was suicidal. I remember reaching a state in the ongoing ordeal where I felt I was right on the edge of a physical and mental breakdown, so I would arise each morning and think to myself, "If an ant crosses my pathway today, then I'm packing it in." In other words, I felt that I could barely get through each day by supporting the crushing load of my wretched, miserable life; therefore, if I had to deal with *anything* extra—even something as seemingly insignificant as an ant crossing my path—it would be enough to cause me to collapse.

I know it was only by God's grace that I persevered through this trying period, but the vital point I am making is this: I believe God *wants* us to break down during hard times—not in the sense of committing suicide, of course. But He wants us to break down in ways that cause our pride, our dogmatism, our hardness of heart and our perceived sufficiency to crumble.

It might be helpful to remember that all those who are ultimately lost in this world will be condemned—not because they disobeyed God's commandments—but, rather, because they rejected His grace. In other words, all who are ultimately lost are those who *refuse to be broken*. They refuse to be brought to the point where they cry out to God from their hearts; therefore, they experience no need of the infinite grace that He offers: "They do not cry out to me from their hearts but wail on their beds" (Hosea 7:14). As I stated in the previous chapter, we are far more comfortable moaning and groaning and griping and complaining about everything that is wrong in our lives ("wailing on our beds") than crying out to God and placing the total weight of our desperate need upon Him.

I worked in mental health case management for about five years, and I can tell you from firsthand experience that most people will cling to their autonomy *at all costs*, and they will justify their independence through the most confounded reasoning and rationalizations. But I do not have to look to the lives of those whom I served during my years in mental health case management to know this, for I find the same reality played out in my own life as well.

God seeks to bring us to the place where we can see this tendency—really *see* it—not only in others but in ourselves as well. The dishonest condition of our unredeemed hearts must change if we are to experience God's deliverance during the difficult times in our lives. Truly, we are no different than the stiff-necked people we see in God's Word. Therefore, like them, we must be broken of our tendency to rationalize, to blame, to murmur, and to complain. In short, we must be brought to the point where we *acknowledge the truth*—however humbling this may be to our proud, arrogant natures. *This* is the key to our deliverance.

I realize that such an analysis may seem overly simplistic, for there are people in all parts of the world who are experiencing life-threatening crises—even extreme abuse. Do I mean to imply that these people could be delivered from these situations by a simple acknowledgment of truth?

Yes, I mean to imply this.

I do not mean to imply that deliverance will necessarily involve a magical escape from the trying circumstances they are experiencing, but it surely *will* involve the reception of needed grace to bear the ordeal as good soldiers of the cross—and this is what God's deliverance is all about. It is about receiving supernatural grace and strength that allow us to move forward in faith rather than be crushed by the circumstances of our lives.

If you doubt the truth of what I am writing, then allow me to ask the following questions:

- Do we believe that the salvation God has wrought for us in Christ allows us to rise above the circumstances in our daily lives—however extreme they may be?

- Do we further believe that this salvation is given freely as a gift rather than as wages we must earn?

This is one area where the rubber meets the road. We must ask ourselves if we *truly believe* that God's salvation in Christ is a gift that allows us to rise above the trying circumstances of our lives. It is only when we believe this about God's salvation that we can truthfully assert that God's grace in Christ is sufficient for us.

Consider two declarations of our Savior that promise victory and peace:

- "Peace I leave with you; my peace I give to you. I do not give to you as the world gives. Do not let your hearts be troubled and do not be afraid" (John 14:27).

- "In this world you will have trouble. But take heart! I have overcome the world" (John 16:33).

Remember, Jesus spoke these promises to His disciples at a time when He was fully aware of the mocking, torture and death that awaited all of them. If we do not believe God's grace in Christ is sufficient for us, then, clearly, we do not believe these promises are true. We are therefore left in a position where the problems in our lives will eventually overwhelm us.

To repeat, the acknowledgment of truth—truth about our situation, truth about God, truth about the condition of our hearts—is the central key to deliverance from the trying circumstances of our lives. This acknowledgment of truth brings us in touch with reality, and when we are brought in touch with reality, we are likewise brought in touch with the one true God who created and structures reality.

It should not be surprising to us that deliverance from crises and extremities requires an acknowledgement of truth, for our Savior makes truth a central theme in His discourses. He states, for example, that legitimate worship of God is worship "in spirit and in truth" (John 4:23, KJV). He also states that He came to this world to "testify to the truth" (John 18:37) and that the only ones who listen to Him are those who are "on the side of truth" (John 18:37). So, again, it should not be surprising that deliverance from trying circumstances requires an acknowledgement of truth.

- We must begin to see the *situations in our lives* truthfully.
- We must begin to see *God* truthfully.
- We must begin to see the *condition of our hearts* truthfully.

These are the primary objectives that God seeks to accomplish by allowing difficult times in our lives. He works through these times to accomplish deliverance from the projection and denial (the "blame game") that come so naturally to us in our fallen state of sin (Genesis 3:12, 13). Once this spiritual deliverance is accomplished, the practical deliverance from the relevant crisis is assured.

The major obstacle to the acknowledgment of truth for fallen beings like you and me is our comfortable immersion in projection and denial. There are many Bible verses that express this truth about the natural condition of our dishonest hearts:

- "Every way of a man is right in his own eyes, but the LORD weighs the hearts" (Proverbs 21:2, NKJV).

- "The heart is deceitful above all things, and desperately wicked; who can know it?" (Jeremiah 17:9, NKJV)
- "Woe is me, for I am undone! Because I am a man of unclean lips, and I dwell in the midst of a people of unclean lips; for my eyes have seen the King, the LORD of hosts" (Isaiah 6:5, NKJV).

The words quoted in the last text are those of Isaiah—a man called to be a mighty prophet of God during a rebellious time in the history of Israel. We see that even this man who was called to be a holy prophet refers to himself as a man of "unclean lips" (that is, a liar) when brought into the presence of the Almighty. This reinforces the point that the major obstacle to the acknowledgment of truth for fallen beings like you and me is our comfortable immersion in a state of denial. Our immersion in this state causes an activity like lying to come quite naturally to us since we are primarily concerned with justifying ourselves rather than confessing the truth.

Have you ever heard the phrase, "the white elephant in the living room"? This is a phrase used to refer to the atmosphere of projection and denial that engulfs dysfunctional families when one or more members are ensnared by some sort of addictive behavior. There is a sense of awkwardness and tension in such families because they are not facing the issues in their lives with honesty and truthfulness. If you were to walk into the home of such a family, you would feel a sense of extreme distance and alienation—as if everyone were "out of touch" with no real feeling of interpersonal connection.

> Everyone is *"out of touch." This is so because each person is involved in an elaborate system of defense and avoidance.*

And, indeed, *everyone is* "out of touch." This is so because each person is involved in an elaborate system of defense and avoidance. The sense of awkwardness and tension that results from this ongoing dishonesty comes across to others like a "white elephant in the living room."

Yet, life goes on for such families as if the "white elephant" (namely, the interpersonal awkwardness and disconnection) were not there. Everyone avoids it. No one wants to talk about it. Everyone learns behaviors and avoidance mechanisms that allow him or her to persevere with a dishonest life.

Why do I mention this now? Because *this* is the point that you and I will reach if we think God expects us to prove something to Him by "gutting it out" during the crises of our lives. We will reach this point because—like the members of the dysfunctional family—we will be thinking thoughts like, *I've got to make it through this. I've got to be strong. I can't break down. If I break down, then everything will come apart at the seams.* In short, we will be trying to *preserve* the very defensive structures in our lives that God is trying to *eliminate*. (I can assure you that this posture of defense and self-protection is the precise posture adopted by works-oriented Christians.)

If we *do* break down, then, in many ways, everything *will* come apart at the seams. But this "coming apart at the seams" is just what is needed, for it will result in the breaking down of our rigid, self-protective defense mechanisms. And this will open the door for a sense of honesty and truthfulness about our situation. And this sense of honesty and truthfulness will usher us into a realm of authentic communication—with others, with ourselves, and with God. We will become aware of our dependency upon Christ in ways of which we were formally oblivious. We will begin to realize—possibly for the first time—just how deeply we need our Savior, and we will be amazed at the strength from God that flows into our lives as we cry out to Him from desperate, needy hearts.

I can testify to the truth of this process from my own personal experience. I remember how self-sufficient I felt before I bottomed out. Even though I would never say something like, "I don't need God," I lived my life as if He did not exist because I had no practical focus or dependence upon Him.

After I bottomed out, however, everything changed. I realized that I needed God *desperately*! I recall sitting on a log in a field after I had completed my doctoral degree and pouring out my heart to Him as I cried. I just couldn't stop crying. I had spent many years acquiring a doctoral degree in a field that prepared me for nothing but teaching philosophy, and now the thought of teaching philosophy was like death to me. So, I was grieving a lost and wasted life.

I would say things to God like, "Can't You see what has happened?"

Yes, God could see what had happened. He saw it coming all along. But He knew that I had to bottom out so the self-protective, defensive structures in my life would come crashing down. Such structures are *always* dishonest and sinful; therefore, they always keep us from acknowledging the truth. For me, these defensive structures took the form of preserving the persona of a doctoral candidate because, deep down, I had no self-confidence, nor did I have any sense that I had accomplished anything worthwhile in my life.

I remember seeing other graduate students progress with their lives while still in graduate school. They married; they had children; they got jobs. I think I was clueless about how to go about doing any of these things because I was so desperately insecure. I clung to my status as a graduate student as if I were a somebody who was going somewhere when there was nothing of substance underneath the false academic veneer.

Once I bottomed out, however, I was no longer concerned about preserving the persona of a doctoral candidate. I knew that, if I didn't get help, I wasn't going to make it. In short, the extremity of my situation broke my stubborn, willful pride, so I got real with myself, with others, and with God. This honesty allowed me to discern important realities about the condition of my heart, and it also allowed me to understand why the crisis happened to me in the first place. It was at this point that I began to experience the genuine flow of living water from the throne of God (John 4:14).

I remember clearly how blinders seemed to fall off my eyes during this time. I began to see all the opportunities that I had squandered because of my defensive arrogance and pride. I also saw the many ways that God had tried to reach me with help during the years I spent in the doctoral program, but my self-protective armor had been just too thick to allow for penetration. I even realized—*finally!*—how I had no reason to expect a different outcome to my many years of study because I had done nothing to properly prepare for employment.

- I had no publications to my credit.
- I had attended no professional meetings.
- I had made no professional inquiries regarding possible positions.

In retrospect, I see that I had quite a smug attitude about such things. I thought of myself as a very qualified philosophical thinker, so I rationalized my negligent course of action by imagining that God would magically plop my "qualified" self into the perfect position when the appropriate time arrived. When I bottomed out, I began to see the truth, and I suddenly felt quite embarrassed and humiliated that I had acted so irresponsibly.

- I was beginning to see the *situation in my life* truthfully.
- I was beginning to see *God* and His care for me truthfully.
- I was beginning to see the *condition of my heart* truthfully.

I will emphasize again that a critical aspect that I needed to understand during the whole process of deliverance was that God was never seeking to punish me for anything through the agency of the crisis, nor was He seeking to test me by observing whether I was able to "gut it out." Rather, God was simply bringing me to the point where I was able to *acknowledge the truth*. And bringing fallen beings like you and me to a point of honestly acknowledging and confessing the truth will always involve *breaking* us—of our pride, our arrogance, and our self-protective defense mechanisms.

If you have any lingering doubt about your need to be broken before you acknowledge the truth, I would invite you to recall the projection and denial in the responses of an "unbroken" Adam and an "unbroken" Eve (Genesis 3:12, 13). When God confronted Adam after his act of rebellion, Adam did not respond by saying, "Boy, I did *just* what you told me not to do." Eve did not respond in this way either. Rather, both gave a convenient explanation—anything but confess!

And remember, Adam and Eve properly represent you and me. The projection and denial that we observe so clearly in *them* come quite naturally—in our fallen state—to *us*.

To summarize, God seeks to bring us to the place where we see that the punishment we deserve as well as the work we need to perform were accomplished *for* us in the person of Jesus. He desires that we rest in this place of grace so that we can begin to see the truth of our situation. Once we see the truth of our situation—which includes our desperate need of His mercy—He desires that we trust Him to deliver us for the sake of His Son.

"Deliverance belongs to the Lord" (Jonah 2:9, RSV).

* * *

Praise God from whom all blessings flow.

Chapter 4
We Are Accepted in Christ

*To the praise of the glory of His grace,
By which He made us accepted in the Beloved.*

(Ephesians 1:6, NKJV)

There is one biblical truth that towers above all others. It is the truth that, once we confess our great need of salvation and trust in Christ as our Savior, we are fully accepted by God in the person of His Son.

And we are accepted *as we are—with* our sin.

This truth is so simple that we are in danger of skipping over it in a way that prevents us from realizing its power. We might think, for example, that the truth of our acceptance in Christ is only for newly born spiritual babes and that we, as mature Christians, possess some personal merit before God because we have been fruitful in some mighty work or because we have been obedient to His commands. In short, we may think we have progressed *beyond* acceptance in Christ. But one never progresses beyond this central truth of salvation.

Regarding what it means to be "accepted in the Beloved," it is important to understand that acceptance *in spite of* our sin is not true acceptance.[8] To be accepted in spite of our sin is not true acceptance because we come to God as sinners; therefore, we must know that God accepts us

---

8   Brennan Manning, *Abba's Child* (Colorado Springs: Navpress, 1994), p. 20.

with our sin, not in spite of it. And God does accept us with our sin. This is grace.

I remember once asking a Christian couple the following question: "Do you think God accepts you as you are—with your sin?" The wife quickly answered, "I've always been taught that God *receives* us as we are, but He does not *accept* us that way."

If we think God does not accept us as we are—with our sin—I can assure you that we will have significant interpersonal problems with others (as this wife did). This is so because the way we relate to others is always a direct reflection of the way we relate to ourselves. And if we believe we are unacceptable to our Creator and Redeemer as we are, then, clearly, we are not relating to ourselves in a healthy way. Therefore, we will not relate to *others* in a healthy way.

I will develop this point more fully in the next chapter, but, for now, consider two texts of Scripture that demonstrate God's acceptance of us in Christ *as we are:*

- "For we maintain that a person is justified [or accepted] by faith apart from the works of the law" (Romans 3:28).

- "To the one who does not work but trusts God who justifies [or accepts] the ungodly, their faith is credited as righteousness" (Romans 4:5).

There is also the well-known text that I quoted at the beginning of this chapter: "To the praise of the glory of His grace, by which He made us accepted in the Beloved" (Ephesians 1:6, NKJV).

Despite the clear and forceful way in which the Bible declares our acceptance by God for Jesus' sake, all of us struggle in this area at one time or another. We are especially prone to these struggles during times of crises when we become painfully aware of our past and present shortcomings. This awareness of our shortcomings makes us feel unacceptable to a pure and holy God.

I remember how I struggled in this area when I initially "bottomed out." I was beginning to see the arrogance and pride in my life (as well as the insensitivity and selfishness) since all of this worked its way back to me in the most painful ways through the words and actions of others. Because I was beginning to see all of this in raw and intense ways, I felt *totally* unacceptable. And this feeling of unacceptability drove me to sin. It became a vicious cycle of (1) unacceptability, (2) sin, (3) greater unacceptability, and (4) greater sin.

The more I tried to be acceptable, the more I would fail; and the more I would fail, the more unacceptable I would feel—and on and on it went.

I was such a basket case during this period that I would chew on my hands in ways that I seemed powerless to control. My hands would sometimes bleed as a result. Once, when I was driving, I found myself sitting behind a car at a red light, and I began chewing on my hand. I remember saying to myself, "This is crazy. I'm not going to do this anymore." So, I stopped. Then, in about thirty seconds, I was doing it again—uncontrollably.

Clearly, I was a mess, but God's grace is sufficient for all the messes we become. Unfortunately, I was unable to receive God's healing grace because I was seeking to make myself acceptable through self-conscious efforts to be good rather than by resting in God's acceptance in Christ. I learned firsthand the truth of this spiritual principle: "So I find this *law* at work: Although I want to do good, evil is right there with me . . . making me a *prisoner* of the law of sin at work within me. What a wretched man I am!" (Romans 7:21, 23, 24, emphasis added).

I eventually learned the truth of another principle as well: "There is now no condemnation for those who are in Christ Jesus, because through Christ Jesus the law of the Spirit who gives life has set you free from the law of sin and death" (Romans 8:1, 2).

I will repeat an all-important point: It was only as I *ceased* self-conscious efforts to be good and *rested* in God's acceptance of me in Christ that beneficial fruit began to develop in my life. Regarding this all-important truth of resting in God's acceptance in Christ, I must emphasize that this is an actual *experience*, not a mere mental assent. In other words, no amount of mental gymnastics in an effort to convince myself that I was in right standing with God could substitute for the actual experience of being loved and accepted *as I was* by our merciful Father in Christ. I mention this because there is often an emphasis in our society on positive thinking and affirmations.

This experience of acceptance became real in my life—not because I practiced positive thinking or recited different kinds of affirmations—but, rather, because I was driven to cry out desperately in faith as I was broken of my pride and arrogance. I simply claimed—in a very personal way—the truth of my acceptance in Christ, and God responded to my anguished cry of faith (as He always does) by ushering me into interpersonal communion with Him. I thus knew by experience that I was loved and accepted by God *as I am*, and this experience of love and acceptance provided a rock-solid spiritual foundation for my walk of faith.

It might be helpful if I explain how all of this took place for me. As I have mentioned, I was going through a time of deep depression and despair after I completed my doctoral degree, and I felt lonely and unacceptable. This experience of loneliness and unacceptance was so intense during this time that I spent most days contemplating ways to end my life so that I would no longer have to live with myself.

I should point out that it was during this time that I was in the state of seemingly hopeless bondage to food. I would eat what others would consider a normal meal; then I would immediately binge on a quart or two of ice cream (or some similar indulgence). I was big on stuffing my feelings, and I seemed powerless to do otherwise.

During this same time, I was renting a room in a couple's home, and one of the persons who owned the home was an instrument that God was using to help me see how insensitive I had been for many years. This person seemed to have no feelings at all, and I keenly felt, in a very raw and intense way, all the verbal barbs that the person directed at me. I understood, possibly for the first time, how easy it is to be hard and insensitive to others. I saw myself in the behavior of this person, and I remember crying out to God many times for forgiveness of my past deeds and for grace and strength to be a more Christlike vessel.

One day during this period, I came "home" to my rented room and collapsed on the floor at about three o'clock in the afternoon. The room had no windows, so it was completely dark when the door was shut. I remember kneeling before God in prayer, as I had done many times before. However, there was something different about this time. Possibly the difference was that I had stepped out in faith this day by not stuffing myself with food. Normally I would have no strength to resist such bingeing, but God brought a certain Scripture to my mind as I was out and about during the afternoon hours: "But put on the Lord Jesus Christ, and make no provision for the flesh, to gratify its desires" (Romans 13:14, RSV). God somehow dropped these words into my heart along with the faith to claim them, and I remember receiving peace and strength from Him—enough to get me to my room rather than going to the refrigerator to binge.

As I knelt before God in prayer, I experienced the Holy Spirit drawing from me a flood of confessions as the pride and arrogance of my life came before me in vivid detail. It was a "flow" that engulfed me for hours—until I went to bed at about eight or nine o'clock that evening.

The next morning, I sensed a spiritual strength that I had not felt for many months or possibly even years. This strength was quite noticeable for me because I had grown accustomed to the brokenness in my heart. I remember the amazement I felt because I thought I was no longer capable of experiencing such spiritual power and fortitude from God.

I was thankful!

The imparted strength that I experienced inspired me to fall on my knees at about the same time that afternoon, and the same experience ensued in which the Holy Spirit drew from me a flood of confessions, as the pride and arrogance of my life came before me. It was as if an infected wound had begun to drain, and all the pus was flowing from my bodily tissues. Sometimes the "drainage" was so intense that I honestly thought I would die. I remember thinking that the landlord would enter my room the next morning and find me dead on the floor. Such was the force of finally seeing the personal pride and arrogance of my life in the light of God's purity and holiness.

At one point during this process, I recall pleading with God to take my life. I thought everything would be so much easier this way. Since I finally understood what a complete hypocrite I had been, I was convinced that everyone who knew me would simply think something along the lines of, *Well, I guess he finally saw what an arrogant jerk he was, and it did him in*. In other words, I was convinced that my demise would make perfect sense to all who knew me, so I pleaded with God to take my life. As I was pleading with God in my state of wretchedness, I remember asking Him in the most serious way, "Why would You want to rebuild and restore such a miserable life when it would be so much easier to let me die?"

And then I received His answer: "Because that's the God I AM."

I admit that I am hesitant to share (or even to believe) any "word" of God that is not derived directly from Scripture, but I'll venture to tell you why I believe God spoke to me in this way. First, let me quote a text from His Word: "And so it is written, The first man Adam was made a living soul; the last Adam was made a quickening spirit" (1 Corinthians 15:45, KJV). Personally, I have found that this "quickening" invariably accompanies activity that is genuinely from God. I have experienced it at different times as God has moved upon my spirit to motivate or uplift me in some way, and I experienced *precisely* this spiritual "quickening" with the words, "Because that's the God I AM." Had I not experienced this quickening, then I would have regarded the words as simply a thought that was passing through my mind. The experience of the accompanying spiritual prompt, however, "transformed" these words into a message of hope from the Almighty.

I kept this "appointment" with God every day at the same time (about 3 o'clock in the afternoon), and I soon found myself being led deeply into His Word and other spiritual literature during these periods of emotional and spiritual catharsis. After ten days of these daily appointments, I remember bowing down before God one evening and suddenly experiencing a flood of His grace as He embraced me with His fullness. I felt nothing but love and acceptance as I was on my knees before Him. I was engulfed by this experience for over three hours (until I fell asleep), and I wept the entire time. The painful awareness of pollution and wretchedness was washed away by a flood of living water, and I experienced only acceptance and holy joy.

And *gratitude!*

When I awoke the following morning, I remember thinking, *Whatever happens from here on out, I know there is hope for me.* Truly, this experience of being "accepted in the Beloved" (Ephesians 1:6, NKJV) became the sweetest experience of my life. Really, what experience could be better than love and acceptance by . . . *God?*

Before I proceed, I need to emphasize that we must always test any component of our experience by the clear statements of Scripture. I need to also emphasize that the gospel message of salvation is an objective message about the historical facts of Christ's life, death, and resurrection in our behalf (1 Corinthians 15:1–4). These historical facts are not dependent upon any subjective experience that occurs in the interior lives of believers. One's hope for forgiveness and acceptance is thus grounded in Christ rather than in any personal religious experience.

The fact remains, however, that God has redeemed us in Christ so that we may find acceptance in His presence and enjoy personal communion with Him. Therefore, until we have a firsthand, conscious *experience* of this acceptance and communion, we will remain separated and alienated from the source of our life and hope. We may have deep theological knowledge and strict devotional practices, but apart from a definite *expe-*

rience of acceptance and communion with our merciful Father in heaven, these avail us nothing. They are but empty religious forms, devoid of the life and substance of salvation.

- We must be born into the fellowship of the Father and the Son (1 John 1:3).
- We must taste and see that the Lord is good (Psalm 34:8).
- We must drink of the water that becomes in us a well of water springing up into everlasting life (John 4:14).

In short, we must experience *personal acceptance* as well as *interpersonal communion* with our Father and God, for, truly, this is the goal and objective of salvation: "This is eternal life: that they know you, the only true God, and Jesus Christ, whom you have sent" (John 17:3).

All who genuinely experience this indispensable fruit of salvation will cease to make self-conscious efforts to be better and will rather allow themselves to be loved and accepted *as they are* (not as they believe they should be).[9] I do not mean to imply that those who allow themselves to be loved and accepted as they are will *remain* as they are. On the contrary, all such individuals who are thus planted in God's grace will *grow* in His grace. In this way, they will find themselves progressively sanctified by God's spiritual power. But this progressive sanctification is a growth *in* grace; it is not a growth *into* grace.

> *Truly, anything less than an experience of being loved and accepted as we are amounts to a futile endeavor to grow into the merit and favor of God rather than allowing ourselves to grow in it. And no one who is attempting to grow into grace will ever experience any true growth in grace.*

Truly, anything less than an experience of being loved and accepted *as we are* amounts to a futile endeavor to grow *into* the merit and favor of God rather than allowing

---

9   Brennan Manning, *Ruthless Trust* (New York: HarperCollins, 2000), p. 92.

ourselves to grow *in* it.[10] And no one who is attempting to grow into grace will ever experience any true growth in grace. All who are attempting to grow into grace will remain stagnant Christians year after year. They may be active and even leaders in their respective churches. However, if they do not have a living experience of being loved and accepted by God *as they are* (*with* their sin), they are not growing.

This is a great irony: Those who believe that they are making great strides forward by doing something for God are the very ones who are remaining stagnant, while those who are finding rest in God's love and acceptance are the ones who are not remaining stagnant but, rather, are growing. Why is this? It is because growth occurs only when we can express the deeper issues of our hearts, and we express the deeper issues of our hearts only when we feel safe and free from condemnation. Finally, we feel safe and free from condemnation only when we have a living experience of love and acceptance by God (*as we are, with* our sin).

Truly, growth is an "inside job," and, on some level, we all understand this. That is, on some level, we all realize that growth occurs from the "inside out." We likewise realize that it does not help us to labor from the "outside in" by stuffing our issues while, at the same time, making self-conscious efforts to keep God's commandments.

I was making many "outside-in" efforts in the years leading to my fall and subsequent depression. I have no doubt that I still fall into this mode at times, but I have learned that the ways of God's Spirit lead to an authentic "inside-out" mode of action. Therefore, I always ask God to help me recognize the times when I am acting as a "whitewashed tomb" (Matthew 23:27) through false and hypocritical behavior. As the psalmist cried out: "Search me, O God, and know my heart; try me, and know my anxieties; and see if there is any wicked way in me, and lead me in the way everlasting" (Psalm 139:23-24 NKJV).

I should make one final point before closing this chapter. I often hear brothers or sisters in the church say something like, "I hate being this way," or, "This just isn't me." I have even found myself thinking or saying such things at times. We utter these words for different reasons. We may be going through a difficult ordeal, or we may be occupied with one issue or another in our lives. What I have learned, however, is that nothing will change for the better in terms of healing, restoration and growth in grace until we acknowledge that this *is* who we are. But, more importantly, we

---

10 Hannah Whitall Smith, *The Christian's Secret of a Happy Life*, p. 80.

need to understand that God *accepts* us this way in Christ. That is, God accepts us—not *in spite of* all our "stuff"—but, rather, *with* all our "stuff."

God knows about the many issues in our lives far better than we do, and He wants to reveal the causes of these issues to us. He also wants to heal us, and He will do this. Once He does heal us, then and only then, will we become fit and sanctified vessels to do a mighty work for Him, if that is His will. Yet, it all starts with His acceptance of us *as we are* in Christ. It doesn't start anywhere else. It doesn't start with our growing *into* grace. Rather, it starts with our being planted *in* grace. And being planted *in* grace means that we are accepted *as we are, with* our sin. That's grace!

Have I emphasized this point enough?

I pray that we all will trust our heavenly Father to deal with the issues in our lives as we rest in His grace and acceptance. As we do, we will be amazed at the tender mercy and great insight that He brings to our situations through a childlike dependence and trust.

* * *

Praise God from whom all blessings flow.

Chapter 5
We Never Get Past Acceptance in Christ

*Did you receive the Spirit by the works of the law,
Or by the hearing of faith?*

---

*But that no one is justified by the law in the sight of God is evident,
For "the just shall live by faith."*

(Galatians 3:2, 11)

    I mentioned in the previous chapter that, as Christians, we should never regard the truth of our acceptance in Christ as something that is meant exclusively for newly born spiritual babes. That is, we should never think that we must progress beyond the experience of acceptance to a place where we have our own personal merit before God. As Galatians 3:11 states, "The just shall *live* by faith" (emphasis added).

    I learned the importance of living by faith and, therefore, never progressing beyond acceptance in Christ through a troubling experience that held me in its grip for many years. It was this: I would often react negatively toward others because I was so easily offended. They would either do something (or not do something) or say something (or not say something), and I would experience an intense feeling of anger and offense in the deepest part of me.

In my early years as a Christian, I wasn't too concerned about these feelings because, being spiritually immature, I simply regarded them as raw experiences of "righteous indignation." However, as the years went by, I eventually understood that these experiences represented an intense root of bitterness and resentment. God helped me to see that I was not experiencing "righteous indignation" at all. Rather, I was experiencing personal rage as I felt my pride being wounded or my will being crossed. I began to see how this negative heart response was affecting my relations with others in harmful ways, yet I had no idea how to get "underneath" the experience to rid myself of it.

I went through a period when I would stuff these feelings whenever they arose. Yet, whether in a passive stuffing mode or a free expression mode, I always knew that I was never addressing the root of the problem in my heart. Then I read a book by Brennan Manning, entitled *Abba's Child*.[11]

Manning was once a Catholic priest and has struggled with alcoholism and other issues in his life. He now seeks to share the lessons he has learned during these struggles through his ministry as a Christian author and speaker.

As I read Manning's book, I remember encountering many grace-oriented statements that initially seemed quite wrong to me. I should mention that I am not naturally a merciful or grace-oriented person. On the contrary, I am naturally quite hard-hearted and works-oriented, and God has brought me through many trying experiences to break these tendencies in me.

Anyway, back to Manning and his book.

Manning has struggled mightily with self-hatred, and this struggle has brought him to understand the importance of acceptance. He also understands the importance of honest and authentic behavior among Christians. Thus, he devotes an entire chapter of his book to addressing the *dis*honest and *non*-authentic part of all of us—which he calls "the Impostor." It was in his chapter "The Impostor" that I found many statements that I initially thought were wrong. Some examples of these are as follows:[12]

"The impostor must be . . . accepted and embraced."

"We make friends with the impostor and accept that we are impoverished and broken."

---

[11] Brennan Manning, *Abba's Child* (Colorado Springs: Navpress, 1994).
[12] Manning, pp. 33–48.

"The impostor and I constitute one person."

"Accepting the reality of our sinfulness means accepting our authentic self."[13]

As I stated, when I initially read Manning's book, I simply could not accept the truth of these statements. This is not surprising, however, because, for many years, I was a person who gloried in a struggle within myself that I now see as quite destructive. I would read statements in Scripture like, "If anyone comes to Me and does not hate . . . even his own life, he cannot be My disciple" (Luke 14:26), and I would think that a degree of self-hatred was spiritually quite healthy. I would thus glory in self-hatred. I thought there was much virtue in the sort of thinking in which I would stand apart from myself and regard a part of myself with disdain—even contempt. Self-hatred was, for me, a red badge of courage, a true mark of honor for all Christians who were willing to fight the true fight and walk the true walk.

I have now come to regard the hatred about which Christ is speaking in this text as hatred of the old man of sin (that is, my unredeemed self), who, admittedly, was in full control before I came to Christ. All who are honest must be brought to the point that they relate to their un-redeemed lives apart from Christ with a sense of hatred, for surely these unredeemed lives are lived in complete rebellion to God. If honest people are never repulsed by their unredeemed lives, then no one would ever see the need of redemption, nor would anyone ever come to Christ.

I will show in a later chapter ("Our Sinful Body Is Dead in Christ") that the Bible assures us that, once we are born again in Christ, this unredeemed body of sin is put to death. There is, therefore, no need for redeemed children of God to be wallowing in self-hatred, nor is there any virtue in such thinking. The important point is this: Once we find acceptance in Christ, any continuing self-hatred will do nothing but stunt our growth in grace, and this was the point that Manning was trying to make.

Anyway, back to his book.

After reading statements like the ones I have quoted above, I remember thinking something like, *Boy, this Manning fellow, he offers such a wimp theology. He needs to grow up and be a man.*

Well, maybe I was the one who needed to grow up.

In any event, God has ways to reach all of us, and, as I continued reading (and re-reading) this chapter in Manning's book, God began showing

---

13 Manning, pp. 25, 26.

me how all this related to the personal struggle I was experiencing with bitterness and resentment. He began to make connections between my head and my heart, and He showed me how Manning's approach could help me. Here are some other statements that Manning makes in the same chapter which helped me to tie all of this together.[14] (These statements somehow passed right over my head in my initial perusal of his material.)

"Any facet of the shadow self that we refuse to embrace becomes the enemy and forces us into defensive postures."

"The art of gentleness toward ourselves leads to being gentle with others."

"Hatred of the impostor is actually self-hatred, for the impostor and I constitute one person."

"Contempt for the false self gives vent to hostility, which manifests itself as general irritation—an irritation at the same faults in others that we hate in ourselves."

"Self-hatred always results in some form of self-destructive behavior." [How could it *not?!*]

Manning mentions how Judas could not face his "shadow," whereas Peter could. Peter, he believes, befriended the impostor within, while Judas raged against him, and, for Judas, this raging self-hatred eventually culminated in the most self-destructive of all behaviors, namely, suicide.

I can truthfully testify that once I began to adopt this "kinder, gentler" approach toward myself, I noticed that my interpersonal relations with others changed quickly and dramatically. I was far more accepting of others, far more tolerant of their behavior. As I mentioned in the prior chapter, the way we relate to others is *always* a direct reflection of the way we are relating to ourselves.

I do not mean to imply that I have "arrived," because I still struggle in this area. Nevertheless, I do not experience the same intensity or frequency of this root of bitterness that I formerly experienced so intensely and so frequently. I think I can say that I experienced a miracle—a miracle of grace. And I did nothing. I simply *stopped* doing something.

And what did I stop doing? I stopped beating myself up. I stopped thinking of parts of myself as unacceptable. I finally realized that we never get beyond acceptance in Christ. Indeed, progressing *beyond* acceptance in Christ amounts to "progressing" *beyond* the state of being saved to the state of being lost—and who wants that?

---

14 Manning, pp. 33-48.

Sometimes we hear people of the world say things like, "Don't beat yourself up about it," and we think, "Oh, they're being too soft on sin." We then falsely conclude that we *should* beat ourselves up about things.

First, let's acknowledge the obvious truth that, yes, the world is generally too soft on sin. Despite this obvious truth, however, beating ourselves up about something accomplishes nothing, and there is no virtue in this activity. It simply represents another form of the futile endeavor to grow *into* grace rather than allowing ourselves to grow *in* it. In other words, the berating of ourselves shows that we refuse to rest and to grow in the grace and acceptance that God has *freely given* to us in Christ.

We are especially prone to berate ourselves when we are trying to persevere through difficult times. Personally, I can't begin to tell you how many times I did this when I was "bottoming out." I have no doubt that this was a significant factor in the severity of my subsequent depression since a depressed state of mind results when anger is turned inward. That is, if we repeatedly berate ourselves for anything and everything (as I was doing) and then focus a laser-sharp intensity of anger toward ourselves because of a perceived boneheadedness (as I was also doing)—well, this is a sure-fire way to become severely depressed.

Truly, we must know that this is never God's will for His children. We must know and experience the reality that God sees—not our imperfection—but, rather, Jesus' perfection. He sees—not our impurity—but, rather, Jesus' purity. God sees Jesus' perfection and purity in His children regardless of how sinful and boneheaded we know ourselves to be. It is only by resting in these qualities of our Savior that we can persevere through difficult times in a way that results in healing and growth. We must cease to berate ourselves and instead *rest* in the love and acceptance of God. Only then will our imperfections be miraculously transformed by the power of His grace.

Consider another point that is relevant here. The layout of the sanctuary in the wilderness was built according to the pattern given by God, and it represented the plan of salvation. When an Israelite came into the courtyard of the sanctuary to confess his sin, do you know what he was surrounded by? It was pure white linen. Do you know what this represented? I cannot see how it represented anything but the perfect righteousness of our Savior. So, even when an Israelite fell into sin and subsequently came in repentance to God to confess this sin, he was still surrounded by the tokens of God's acceptance. How else could he "enter His gates with thanksgiving and His courts with praise"? (Psalm 100:4)

Despite these many references in the Bible to our acceptance in Christ, we might still be tempted to think, *Oh, but it's so hard for me to feel accepted when I'm going through a personal crisis in my life—especially one that I know I have brought upon myself.* We might also be tempted to think, *This is an area that was easier for Jesus because He lived a perfect life. He could look back on His life with the satisfaction of knowing that He had pleased His Father and had done His will. He could, therefore, have confidence in His Father's acceptance.* We might conclude by thinking, *If I could look back on a life like that, then I would be able to rest in God's acceptance of me. But my life has been such a mess, and it makes me feel unacceptable.*

> *If God saw anything less than a perfect life in our past, then we would come under condemnation, but the Bible is clear that there is no condemnation for those who have accepted Jesus as their Savior (Romans 8:1).*

When we are troubled by thoughts like these, we need to realize that we are thinking this way only because the ultimate loser, Satan, has convinced us that our past is different than Jesus' past—but it is not (at least, in God's eyes, it is not). And why is our past not different than Jesus' past? Because our justification in Christ means that the Father sees Jesus' life as ours. It means that the Father sees the same perfect life when He looks into *our* past as He does when He looks into Jesus' past. If God saw anything less than a perfect life in our past, then we would come under condemnation, but the Bible is clear that there is *no* condemnation for those who have accepted Jesus as their Savior (Romans 8:1).

Remember, the perfect life that Jesus lived is primarily a *gift* for us to receive, not a *standard* for us to attain. This truth is so central to Scripture and to salvation by grace that it seems superfluous to give Bible texts to support it; nevertheless, I will provide a few.

- "She will give birth to a son, and you are to give him the name Jesus, because he will save his people from their sins" (Matthew 1:21).
- "And all are justified freely by his grace through the redemption that came by Christ Jesus" (Romans 3:24).
- "For it is by grace you have been saved, through faith—and this is not from yourselves, it is the gift of God—not by works, so that no one can boast" (Ephesians 2:8, 9).

At some point we must simply decide whether we truly believe that salvation is by grace (and thus involves the personal reception of a gift) or we believe that salvation is by works (and thus involves the personal achievement of a standard). In short, we must decide whether or not Jesus truly is the Lamb of God given to take away the sin of the world (John 1:29).

I remember when I used to wallow around in my sinfulness and think, *Oh, but I just can't believe that God sees Jesus' life in place of my own.* I finally realized that this reluctance to believe God was not the painful cry of a sensitive soul who was struggling with acceptance; rather, it was the proud murmuring of an arrogant sinner who was enmeshed in spiritual rebellion. God eventually brought me to a place in my life where I was humbled before Him and could accept the gift that He offered to me in the person of His Son.

The vital point we must understand is that each of us can have the same confidence in the Father's acceptance that Jesus had because God is looking at the same life in each case. This is grace, and the entire foundation of our walk of faith is grounded in this knowledge and experience of our acceptance by God in the person of Jesus.

Satan understands that God's acceptance of His children in the person of Jesus is the foundation of all spiritual life and growth. Therefore, he focuses all his efforts on placing uncertainty in our minds about being true sons and daughters of God. You remember how he prefaced his temptations to Jesus with the insinuation of doubt?

"If you are the Son of God . . ." (Matthew 4:2, 6).

Be assured that he will do the same with each of us. That is, he will try to convince us that the desperation of our present circumstance shows that we are not children of God. We will have nothing to fear from the evil one in this area, however, if we simply remember that God did not allow

His Son to be tempted by the devil in the wilderness until He had first given Him His personal assurance of acceptance: "This is my Son, whom I love; with him I am well pleased" (Matthew 3:17).

God will do no less for each of us. He will not lead us into the wilderness to face the temptations of Satan without first giving us this same assurance of acceptance. He understands our desperate need to know that, in Christ, we are welcomed and loved in His sight.

If we attempt to face Satan's temptations without this assurance of acceptance, then each of us will surely fall prey to his insinuations of doubt. Think of how easily Jesus could have doubted His Father's care when He found Himself starving in the desert after forty days. He knew that He had been led there by the Spirit (Mark 1:12). Nevertheless, He was hungry and destitute by the time Satan approached Him. It makes perfect sense, therefore, that the evil one would tempt Him to doubt His Father's provision and to take matters into His own hands: "If you are the Son of God, tell these stones to become bread" (Matthew 4:3).

Satan will do the same with each of us. He will tempt us to doubt our Father's care and to depart from His expressed will in our lives to spare ourselves of the perceived embarrassment of whatever crisis in which we happen to find ourselves. If we are not grounded in an experience of acceptance, then we will surely fall prey to these temptations, for we will be continually harassed by thoughts such as,

- *Would God really allow His beloved child to be in a situation like this?*

- *How can I think God loves me when this disaster has come upon me?*

- *Would a true child of God ever have to face such humiliating circumstances?*

And on and on.

Indeed, the ultimate loser, Satan, will convince us of a thousand reasons that we should doubt our status as God's children. All these doubts will be powerless, however, once we have truly experienced the voice of God speaking to our souls, "This is my son [or daughter] in Christ, whom I love; with him [or with her] I am well pleased."

I do not mean to imply that we will no longer fall under the power of sin, for all of us have many lessons of faith to learn, and sanctification is the work of a lifetime. But we will no longer fret about our standing before God, and we will no longer concern ourselves about whether we have been abandoned by Him. We will know *by experience* that God is our Father in Christ, and this experience of love and acceptance will keep us grounded to keep us from becoming overwhelmed by guilt and shame.

One final point: Once we are grounded in God's acceptance of us in Christ, we should not begin a process of self-conscious exertion in an ongoing effort to please Him, for our growth in grace depends upon our resting in the assurance that God is perfectly pleased with Jesus. Remember, Jesus lived His perfect life in our behalf, and we cannot add anything to this.

One might say, "But I accepted Jesus many years ago, and I want to grow. Also, I want to be fruitful in ministry, so I make self-conscious efforts to please God." My response to these statements would be, "The only place of growth and fruitful ministry is the place of grace and acceptance in the person of Jesus Christ. Good works flow *only* from this place, and they flow as the *fruit*, not the *root*, of our salvation."

A bit of clarification is probably needed.

When I refer to the root of our salvation, I refer to our acceptance by God in the person of His Son. The only works and obedience that are relevant here are those of our Savior, Jesus, and these are already completed in our behalf.

When I refer to the fruit of our salvation, I refer to all that flows from this redemptive place of acceptance. So, the works that spring forth as the fruit of our salvation are never self-conscious efforts to do good, for such works imply an exertion to reach a standard—and the only standard that is relevant has already been fully attained in our behalf by Jesus. So, the works that spring forth as the fruit of our salvation are—not self-conscious efforts to do good—but, rather, acts that flow spontaneously from a heart of gratitude that has been renewed by God's redeeming grace. This is the central characteristic of fruitful Christians: gratitude and praise. It is never grunting and self-exertion.

Would you allow me to repeat this truth?

- The central characteristic of fruitful Christians is always gratitude and praise; it is never grunting and self-exertion.

Think of the matter in this way: We do not want to be "whitewashed tombs" like the Pharisees of Jesus' day, do we? (Matthew 23:27). But how would we be any different than the Pharisees of Jesus' day if we are enmeshed in an ordeal of gritting our teeth and buckling down to a "religious" routine of self-conscious effort? Is this the picture of someone with a renewed heart who is a new creation in Christ? (2 Corinthians 5:17)

I have personally found that all self-conscious effort to do good involves a stepping outside the cleft of the Rock (that is, our place of rest and acceptance in Christ—Exodus 33:22). Whenever I am involved in such effort, my carnal self immediately begins thinking thoughts like, *Hey, look at me! Look at all this good stuff I'm doing!* I am already falling from grace when I am in a condition such as this.

> *So, what do we do when we don't feel like doing what we know we ought to do?*

So, what do we do when we don't feel like doing what we know we ought to do? These are the times when we, as Christians, often buckle down to a routine of self-conscious effort and exertion, but I would say that such times are a call to *confession*, not a call to self-conscious effort or exertion.

Think about it: If we do not feel like doing something we know we ought to do, then something is wrong with our hearts, right? No amount of grunting or self-conscious effort will cure this. On the contrary, any self-conscious effort or routine of mechanical works will probably cause the heart issue to become worse since we will begin to feel resentment about having to do something that we have no desire to do. At times such as these, we need healing and restoration, and the first step in this process is always a confession of need. We simply confess to God that our hearts are woeful and wretched before Him, and we cry out for mercy, insight, and strength.

I have done this repeatedly when I have found myself in such situations. I never try to "gut it out" during such periods because I know that such a posture will accomplish nothing. Instead, I seek to obtain grace, wisdom, and fortitude from God, for I know that I am in desperate need of healing and discernment. As the psalmist wrote: "I will run the way of thy commandments, when thou shalt enlarge my heart" (Psalm 119:32, KJV). This is the crucial point: My heart needs to be "enlarged" so that it will respond properly to God's call.

Recall these important words of Scripture: "So then, just as you received Christ Jesus as Lord, continue to live your lives in him" (Colossians 2:6).

How did we receive Christ Jesus? Did we receive Him by a lot of personal resolve and exertion, by buckling down to a lot of self-conscious effort? Or did we receive Him by admitting our helplessness and then confessing our need? We received Jesus by admitting our helplessness and then confessing our need, right? God's Word says, "So . . . continue to live your lives in him."

I realize that our reception of Jesus also involved an important step of faith, but this step of faith did not involve self-conscious effort. It simply amounted to an act of trust whereby we took God at His word and thus believed that we were truly loved and accepted by Him in the person of His Son.

The key to victory is to abide in this place of acceptance. That is, the key to victory is to refrain from all self-conscious effort and, rather, allow ourselves to be loved and accepted by God as we are in Christ. This place of rest and acceptance puts us in a posture toward God that allows us to be inspired to purity of heart and to bountiful acts of service. This flows as the *fruit* of our salvation that is *already secure* in Christ. It does not flow as the result of self-conscious effort to attain a certain standard.

If we ever feel that we are not inspired to purity of heart and charitable acts of service (and, of course, there will be times such as these), then we should confess this truth to God rather than grit our teeth and make self-conscious efforts to "gut it out." The Holy Spirit will respond to this honest confession by revealing to us the heart issues that are preventing the living water from flowing freely in our lives. He will work on this heart level to bring the matter to resolution. He will not work through some robotic, mechanical routine in our outer lives.

But we must know that we are fully accepted in God's sight throughout the entire process—regardless of how much pollution in our wretched hearts rises to the surface during the ordeal.

Remember—

We Never Get Past Acceptance in Christ!

* * *

Praise God from whom all blessings flow.

Chapter 6

We Have Obeyed God's Commandments in Christ, Part 1

*Christ is the culmination of the law
So that there may be righteousness for everyone who believes.*

(Romans 10:4)

All of us who have accepted Jesus as our Savior have a desperate need to know that we have been given a life of perfect obedience as a gift. Since we have been given this gift, we have, in God's sight, obeyed His commandments perfectly in the person of His Son. We also have a desperate need to know that we cannot add anything to what Jesus has already accomplished in this area. That is, we cannot obey God's commandments in a way that supplements what He has already done *for* us. We must simply rest in the obedience that we have been given.

I realize that all of us know, on some level, that we are saved by grace and not by works. For this reason, we would never say something like, "I'm trying to add to what Christ has done for me." Nevertheless, although we would never say something so openly legalistic and works-oriented, we often live our lives in openly legalistic and works-oriented ways because we become confused about the concepts I mentioned in the previous chapter—namely, the root and the fruit of our salvation.

An important point about the root and the fruit of our salvation is this: God's grace is always the root, and our good works are always the fruit. Stated differently, our salvation is never rooted in our good works; rather, it is always rooted in Christ's good works. I do not mean to imply by this that the fruit of our lives is not important because clearly it is, and I know we understand this. Christ Himself declares plainly: "Every good tree bears good fruit" (Matthew 7:17). So, again, the fruit of our lives is important.

When considering the fruit of a person's life, however, we must consider carefully Christ's parable of the man who sows good seed in his field (Matthew 13:24–30, 36–43). We see in this parable that a man sows seeds of wheat, but an enemy sows weeds. Jesus explains that the seeds producing wheat represent sons of the kingdom, while the seeds producing weeds represent sons of the evil one (Matthew 13:38). He does not, however, give a definitive test that allows one to differentiate the one from the other. That is, He does not say, "Here is an infallible way to determine if a plant is a sprout of wheat or a sprout of a weed." Rather, He cautions *against* any such evaluation before the harvest, for He states that *only at the time of the harvest* will the fruit of all lives be properly manifested for final evaluation.

The relevant point we need to understand is this: It is only at the end of our lives that our fruit can be infallibly evaluated by another. This is so because we all go through times in our walk of faith when we stumble and fall. We make mistakes. We disobey God. There are times when each of us enjoys the pleasures of sin for a season, and there are also times when we are not able to see to the other side of seemingly hopeless bondage.

I was in a position like this when I initially became depressed. I was just so weak during this phase of my life, and there were times when I saw no hope of deliverance. During these hopeless periods, I did not have eyes of faith to see to the other side of my extremity, so I could not imagine a time when the things of God would once again become the source of life and hope for me. Sinful indulgence was thus my only form of release and escape.

But God understood my weakness during this time, and He restored me despite my many lapses into unbelief. He will do no less for you. He knows that you and I are weak and have many lessons to learn. He does not cast us off because we are imperfect, faithless children. He always relates to us through a heart that is overflowing with infinite tenderness and compassion. Nevertheless, if someone were sent to evaluate my life during this period to determine if I was a maturing sprout of wheat or a weed—well, I think I know what the verdict would have been. For this reason, we must always remember that, although the fruit of our lives is clearly important, none of us is ever in a position in this life to infallibly differentiate between a heart that is open to God's truth and one that isn't.

Returning to the concepts of the root and the fruit of our salvation, even though God invariably relates to us through His unfailing mercy and love, we will have no basis for assurance in our walk of faith if we are confused about these two concepts. Indeed, if we ever think that the basis of our assurance with God is the fruit of our lives, then our spiritual foundation is nothing more than our record of good works—and how solid is that?

Not solid at all.

The point we need to understand is that God does not want us to be looking to His commandments, nor does He want us to be thinking about how obedient we are in keeping them. His commandments are not our Savior; Christ is. Therefore, we should be looking to Him, not to a set of cold, legalistic abstractions of God's moral nature.

What kind of persons do you think we will become if we are always looking to God's commandments and to our supposed obedience to them? How much gratitude do you think we will experience while engaged in this activity? How much compassion and spiritual rest? We need to be looking—not to God's commandments—but, rather, to the person who has *kept* these commandments *perfectly* in our behalf.

The Bible is clear that the function of God's law (that is, the Ten Commandments) is to convict us of sin (Romans 3:20) and thus lead us to Christ (Galatians 3:24). The Bible never places the law before believers as a standard that they must reach to be approved or accepted by God. In fact, the Bible is clear that the only thing that any of us will ever get from the law is

CONDEMNATION.

I do not mean to imply by this statement that God's Ten Commandment law is not the standard for our salvation, because it surely is. My only point is that since Jesus has kept every commandment of the law perfectly in our behalf, we have already met the one standard that God imposes. So, by faith in Jesus as our Savior, we are justified in God's sight, and we will never arrive at this justification in any other way. That is, we will never get any approval or acceptance by thinking of *ourselves* in relation to God's law. We get this approval and acceptance only by thinking of *Jesus* in relation to God's law. If we think we are getting approval or acceptance by thinking of ourselves in relation to God's law, it is because we have no conception of our heavenly Father's holy and exalted character and are thus deeply deceived.

The books of Romans and Galatians are filled with passages that confirm the true functions of God's law—namely, to convict us of sin and thus lead us to Christ:

- "Therefore no one will be declared righteous in God's sight by the works of the law; rather, through the law we become conscious of our sin" (Romans 3:20).

- "For we maintain that a person is justified by faith apart from the works of law" (Romans 3:28).

- "The law brings wrath" (Romans 4:15).

- "A person is not justified by the works of the law, but by faith in Jesus Christ" (Galatians 2:16).

- "The law was our guardian until Christ came that we might be justified by faith" (Galatians 3:24).

God's Word thus states in the plainest language that the law functions—not to justify us before God—but, rather, to bring us to a knowledge of sin and therefore lead us to Jesus Christ, our Savior from sin. But the Bible does not merely assert that we cannot be justified by works of the law; it also asserts that all who endeavor to do this are cursed: "For all who rely on the works of the law are under a curse, as it is written: 'Cursed is everyone who does not *continue* to do everything written in the Book of the Law' (emphasis added)" (Galatians 3:10).

At one time in my Christian walk I would have responded to a Scripture text like this by proudly stating, "I am not cursed by the law because I am not merely a *hearer* of the law; rather, I am a *doer*." It took a hard time or two to break such delusion in me and to allow me to recognize the truth of yet another passage of Scripture:

> Now you, if you call yourself a [Christian]; if you rely on the law and boast in God; if you know his will and approve of what is superior because you are instructed by the law; if you are convinced that you are a guide for the blind, a light for those who are in the dark, an instructor of the foolish, a teacher of little children, because you have in the law the embodiment of knowledge and truth—you, then, who teach others, do you not teach yourself? You who preach against stealing, do you steal? You who say that people should not commit adultery, do you commit adultery? . . . You who boast in the law, do you dishonor God by breaking the law? As it is written: "God's name is blasphemed [in the world] because of you" (Romans 2:17–24).

(I have merely substituted the word "Christian" for "Jew" in verse 17 and the phrase "in the world" for the phrase "among the Gentiles" in verse 24.)

I have learned that whenever I am in some supposedly obedient, "keeping-the-law" mode, then I am not allowing God to deal with the real issues of my heart. Like the Jews of Paul's day, I am in bondage and denial. I now try to ask myself the same question that the Word of God asks, "You who boast in the law, do you dishonor God by breaking the law?" (Romans 3:23)

Do I?

If I ever think I am *not* dishonoring God by breaking His law, then I simply re-read the Sermon on the Mount (Matthew 5–7). I then realize that, if I feel a twinge of anger, I am guilty of murder (Matthew 5:22). If I feel a taint of lust, I am guilty of adultery (Matthew 5:28). And if I experience a moment of unbelief, I am guilty of idolatry (Matthew 6:24; Romans 14:23). In short, I realize that I could never be one who boasts in God's law without dishonoring Him by breaking it. Indeed, the Bible states plainly that God gave His law for the very reason of silencing all mouths like mine. He brings each of us to the point of seeing his or her desperate need of His mercy: "Now we know that whatever the law says, it says to those who are under the law, so that every mouth may be silenced and the whole world held accountable to God" (Romans 3:19).

So, is my mouth silenced? This is the only question I need to ask when it comes to God's law.

A vital point to remember regarding our relation to God's law is this: None of us will ever progress beyond a place of desperate need. That is, neither you nor I will ever get to the point of being able to say, "I'm beyond the point of needing God's mercy. I'm now into obediently keeping His law." In short, neither you nor I will ever reach a point of "holy flesh" because, as long as we are in this body of sin and death, the presence of sin is a reality in our lives, and sin's presence taints all the thoughts and actions that flow from our sinful selves.

If we are inclined to dismiss "minor" infractions, such as experiencing anger or lust, then we are *really* in denial. That is, if we think that experiences such as these do not amount to a breaking of God's law, then we are very, very deceived. And why is this? Because we seem to have no sense of how the providences of God's grace have protected us from doing things in our lives that we otherwise would have done. We all need to have a true sense of this reality and to understand that it is only because we were hedged in by divinely ordained circumstances that our anger did not result in murder and our lust did not result in adultery. We must understand that, if we had *not* been hedged in by these circumstances and thus protected by God's grace, our anger surely *would* have resulted in murder, and our lust, in adultery.

This preserving activity of God is especially true for us when we are enduring trying circumstances. His hand is over us to protect us in a hundred different ways during such crises because He knows how weak and vulnerable we are at such times. We need to rest in these divine providences during the hard times of life, knowing that, as sons and daughters of God, we are worthy of God's protection and care by virtue of the perfectly obedient life of His Son.

A relevant point here is this: "Circumcision is circumcision of the heart, by the Spirit, not by the written code" (Romans 2:29). Since true circumcision is of the heart and not the flesh, and since it is affected by the Spirit and not the written code, then all those with uncircumcised hearts are lawbreakers. It doesn't matter that anger or lust is stuffed by religious Pharisees and, therefore, finds no expression in observable outward actions. The core issue is the same as when our anger or lust does find expression, for the core issue is a polluted, uncircumcised heart.

If we understand that the real issue in salvation is an issue of the heart, then we will likewise understand that we are never dealing with this central heart issue if we are conscious of being outwardly obedient to God by keeping His commandments. What good is accomplished by robotic, outward obedience if our hearts are lusting after the things of the world?

How can we possibly be healed and restored while remaining in a deceived condition such as this? Salvation is an "inside" job, and the Holy Spirit always works from the inside out, not the outside in. Satan is the one who works from the outside in. He entices us from the outside through our five senses to work inwardly and corrupt the heart.

Instead of trying to gain assurance by focusing on the fruit of our salvation, we should rather focus on the root of it—and the root of it is always God's grace in Christ. Therefore, if we are to possess true assurance of salvation—whether during a crisis or not—we need to know that we are truly abiding in Christ. Once we know this, we will have all the assurance we need. (In chapter 10, "We Are Born Again in Christ," I examine the criteria the Bible gives so that we may know we are truly born-again children of God.)

I will now make one final point about God's law and the faith of salvation. Consider this Bible passage: "Do we, then, nullify the law by this faith? Not at all! Rather, we uphold the law" (Romans 3:31). This is a favorite text of legalistic Christians, and I have heard it quoted many times to justify an unbiblical, graceless emphasis upon God's law. We must ask ourselves: What does this text mean? And why did Inspiration move Paul to write something about "upholding" (NIV) or "establishing" (KJV) God's law in his epistle to the Romans?

For those of you who have read Paul's epistle to the Romans, you know that the author was focused upon salvation by grace through faith. Therefore, as you might imagine, I do not think Paul intended to say, "Yes, we are saved by God's grace through faith in Christ, so now we should set our minds to keeping God's law because His law is now established." I honestly cannot imagine that anyone would think that this is what Paul meant if he or she read the entire book of Romans with an honest and unbiased heart.

What Paul is stating in context is that the only way for God's law to be truly upheld or established is for us to acknowledge, once and for all, that we are law-*breakers*, and we thus have a desperate need for a perfect law-*keeper*—namely, Jesus Christ. In other words, only our mighty Savior, Jesus, kept God's commandments perfectly. Therefore, God's law is established and upheld as the perfect standard for salvation only when salvation is by grace through faith in Him. We must, therefore, place our faith in our Savior and not in ourselves to be the perfect keeper of God's law.

Think of the matter in this way: Those who think that God's law is "established" because they are now keeping it—well, these persons are not establishing God's law at all. On the contrary, they are trampling upon it, for they are breaking it repeatedly through their anger, their lust, their impatience, their intemperance, their unbelief . . . and on and on. They simply allow themselves to remain conveniently in denial about this truth, but it is true nonetheless.

It is only Jesus who kept God's law by a life of perfect obedience. Therefore, it is only when we acknowledge that we are lawbreakers (not law-keepers) who are in need of the grace that we find through faith in Him that God's law is truly established and upheld.

Our real need is not the law but, rather, the Spirit: "Now the Lord is the Spirit, and where the Spirit of the Lord is, there is freedom" (2 Corinthians 3:17). In other words, we need the

> *Those who think that God's law is "established" because they are now keeping it—well, these persons are not establishing God's law at all.*

freedom that the Spirit of God gives us through faith in the perfect law-keeping of Christ. We do not need the bondage that the letter of the law gives us through the law-breaking of our flesh (Romans 7:7–24). The freedom of the Spirit arises from the knowledge and experience that we are justified (that is, accepted) as we are—*apart* from any works of the law (Romans 3:28).

This justification in Christ allows us to come out from under the condemnation that we experience during the trying circumstances in our lives. We experience this condemnation because we are weak in spiritual power during such times, and we are acutely aware of this weakness (and sinfulness). Satan thus seeks to discourage us through his accusations and censure. But the freedom of the Spirit provides release from this condemnation so that we can begin to genuinely express what is in our hearts. And when we begin to express what is in our hearts, we experience spiritual growth (as we will see in later chapters).

* * *

Praise God from whom all blessings flow.

Chapter 7
We Have Obeyed God's Commandments in Christ, Part 2

Now if the ministry that brought death,
Which was engraved in letters on stone, came with glory,

. . .

Will not the ministry of the Spirit be even more glorious?
If the ministry that brought condemnation was glorious,
How much more glorious is the ministry that brings righteousness!

(2 Corinthians 3:7, 9)

I will state something at the start of this chapter that will doubtless be controversial. Here it is: If we are in a mode of "obediently keeping God's law," then we are spiritually frozen. That is, we are not growing.

One might wonder how I can be so sure about this. One might even openly disagree by stating, "God has given His commandments for a reason. He does not want His children to be lying, cheating, stealing, murdering or committing adultery. Therefore, all of us should be in an obedient mode of keeping God's law."

I would certainly agree that God has given His commandments for a reason, and I would also agree that God does not want His children lying, cheating, stealing, murdering, or committing adultery. I would not agree, however, that this implies that God wants us in a mode of "obediently keeping His law." As I mentioned in the prior chapter, the reason God has given us His commandments is to convict us of sin and to lead us to Christ (Romans 3:20; Galatians 3:24). Therefore, if the law has done its God-appointed work, we have been convicted of sin and have confessed our need of Jesus as our Savior. In other words, we are believers. If we now think that we must be focused upon keeping God's commandments after coming under the care and supervision of the Good Shepherd, then we are deeply confused about the function of these commandments, and we are also confused about the process by which we are sanctified.

We all understand that the law is an ongoing source of objective guidance for those who are unknowingly ignorant or wayward; nevertheless, we must remember Paul's counsel to Timothy whenever we desire to provide guidance to someone through the medium of God's commandments. Paul writes about those who desire to be "teachers of the law" (1 Timothy 1:7), and he states that these have departed from the goal of "love, which comes from a pure heart and a good conscience and a sincere faith" (1 Timothy 1:5). Paul goes on to state that the law is "good" only if one "uses it properly" (1 Timothy 1:8).

And when is God's law used properly? Paul declares that it is used properly—*not* when it is used in relation to believers who desire to be righteous in Christ—but, rather, when it is used in relation to the willfully disobedient. He states: "The law is made *not for the righteous* but for lawbreakers and rebels, the ungodly and sinful, the unholy and irreligious, for those who kill their fathers or mothers, for murderers, for the sexually immoral, for those practicing homosexuality, for slave traders and liars and perjurers—and for whatever else is contrary to the sound doctrine that conforms to the gospel concerning the glory of the blessed God" (1 Timothy1:9 –11, emphasis added). Clearly, I am not primarily concerned with this group because it comprises precisely the people who need to be convicted of sin and led to Christ—which is the *God-appointed function of the law*. In this chapter, I am primarily concerned about the mode in which we, as believers, must abide to grow spiritually, and this mode is definitely *not* a law-centered one.

First, the Bible is clear that the focus of God's law is the old man of sin, not the new creation in Christ (Romans 7:10). The Bible is also clear that the function of God's law is to convict and to execute this rebellious entity (Romans 7:11). The old man of sin is simply who we were before we were born again as new creations in Christ. It is the proud, stubborn self that wants to be the master of its own destiny. The function of the law is to bring all of us to the point of seeing our identity as the rebellious beast that it is. We thus realize that it must be put to death so the new creation in Christ can be the operative force in our lives.

The chain of events normally goes something like this: We see the truth and justice embodied in God's commandments, so we try to keep His law. We eventually realize, however, that we can't do this. So, if we are honest, we cry out for deliverance and salvation, which God has provided in the person of His Son. God then recreates us through the experience of the new birth (which I will cover in a later chapter).

The important point is that, once we are born again, we do not stay in the striving mode of trying to keep God's law, but, rather, we *rest* in God's acceptance of us in Christ. Indeed, for as long as we remain in the striving mode of trying to keep God's law, just so long will we remain in the state that Paul describes in Romans 7:21: "So I find this law at work: Although I want to do good, evil is right there with me."

Notice that Paul states this is a *law*. He does not state something wishy-washy like, "Boy, sometimes when I want to do good, I find that I'm too weak to do it." No, he writes something much stronger. He says that he finds a *law* at work that, when he wants to do good, evil is right there with him (Roman 7:21). He goes on to state that this "law" makes him a *prisoner* of the law of sin at work within him (Roman 7:23). Finally, he cries out, "What a wretched man I am!" (Romans 7:24).

So, what is Paul's solution? "There is now no condemnation for those who are in Christ Jesus, for through Christ Jesus the law of the Spirit who gives life has set you free from the law of sin and death" (Romans 8:1, 2). In short, Paul's solution is *acceptance*. Paul wants each of us to see that we are accepted by God because we have accepted His Son, Jesus, as our Savior. We can now *cease* our self-conscious efforts to do good and instead *rest* in God's acceptance of us in Christ. As we do this, beneficial fruit will be produced in our lives.

These experiences of rest and acceptance need to be spiritual realities in our lives. We need to *experience* rest, and we need to *experience* acceptance. We will experience these realities when we have been born into His family and have thus tasted that He is good.

Returning to the question of how one could know that someone who is in the mode of "obediently keeping God's law" is spiritually frozen and thus not growing, one can know this is true because, as I also mentioned previously, growth occurs only when a person is able to rest in the full assurance of acceptance in Christ. You will recall that it is only such rest in the assurance of full acceptance that allows us to feel safe and free from condemnation. And it is only when we feel safe and free from condemnation that we allow ourselves to express the deeper issues of our hearts. Finally, it is only when we express the deeper issues of our hearts that we grow.

Just as growth results when we feel safe to express the deeper issues of our hearts, so does stagnation and lack of growth result when we do *not* feel safe to express the deeper issues of our hearts. And we surely do not feel safe expressing these deeper heart issues when we feel we must be focused upon keeping God's law. When we are focused upon keeping God's law, we are invariably suppressing the significant issues in our personal lives. This is so because the only thing we get from God's law is condemnation. We never get acceptance or comfort from God's law, and if people believe that they *do* get these things from God's law, it is only because they are deeply deceived about the wretched state of their polluted heart.

Since we get only condemnation from God's law, anyone who is focusing upon this law is therefore feeling condemned all the time. How can anyone grow in a state such as this? The law-focused person will either be stuffing these feelings of condemnation—in which case he or she will be frozen behind a wall of self-defense and denial—or the person will be trying somehow to face these feelings honestly—in which case he or she will be frozen by waves of guilt, shame, and despair. In short, we never feel free to express the deep issues of our hearts (or even to *know* them) when we feel we must conform our behavior to a cold, external constraint like God's law.

The sad irony is this: It is the suppression of the deep issues of our hearts that ultimately results in law-breaking behavior (which is, of course, the very behavior we are seeking to avoid). The suppression of the issues of the heart keeps them from coming to the surface where God can reveal them to us and begin our healing. It is only through God's supernatural process of healing that our outward behavior eventually comes into conformity with His commandments.

If we are honest with ourselves, we will acknowledge that we have a desperate need, not for a bunch of rules and regulations, but, rather, for healing and restoration. Indeed, when it comes to rules and regulations, the Bible refers to such an "old covenant" approach as a ministry of condemnation and death (2 Corinthians 3:7, 9). So, how could reasonable people think that such an approach would bring spiritual life and growth? Consider a child living in a home with many rules and regulations. Imagine that the child has some "issues" (as all of us do), causing him to occasionally experience feelings of fear and insecurity (again, as all of us do). He might even experience feelings of anger and resentment. Now imagine that the child acts as if everything is fine and conducts himself in a very prim and proper manner whenever he is at home with his father. Why would the child do this? He would do this because his father has "laid down the law." His father has made it clear what his expectations are. So, the child stuffs his true feelings and lives a false life as a whitewashed tomb. This is *my* story, and I have no doubt that, in one way or another, it is the story of many others as well.

My father had his personal struggles, and these struggles led him to be the type of father he was. I know he did the best he could, especially considering that his wife (my mother) died when I was a year old and my sister was three. He suddenly found himself jobless with no wife and two small children. Yet, he managed to keep our family together through some very difficult years. I remember asking him once, when I was older, why he was never around when my sister and I were younger. He said, "Stuart, if I came home, I would think, and I couldn't think."

My father was not the reflective type at all, so this was doubtless his way of saying that, if he spent any amount of time at home with my sister and me, he would begin to reflect upon our desperate situation and would become overwhelmed and depressed. When he did spend time at home, however, the atmosphere that he perpetuated in our rented apartments was one of rigid rules and regulations with no room for honest sharing. I never realized how deeply I was affected by this atmosphere until decades in my life had passed. I then began to understand that my defensive structures had become so rigid that I seemed incapable of communicating honestly about my needs and desires. I was such a poser, but I never realized this about myself until the proud inertia of my dishonest, defensive life was broken by heart-wrenching trials.

My inability to express my true needs and desires was so pronounced that I did not have a clue about what I should do when I graduated from college. I knew what I *wanted* to do, but I honestly felt helpless to pursue the path of my desires, and I stayed in this mode for years (decades, really).

I shared this lack of fulfillment with a therapist once when I was feeling overwhelmed with my dishonesty. I remember her asking me, "So, Stuart, what would happen in your home when you would try to pursue—or even to express—your dreams?" This was a real breakthrough for me in understanding how deeply we can be wounded, for I remember how brutally my father would respond to any honest sharing of thoughts or ideas. He usually responded with mocking sarcasm that resulted in open humiliation. The realization helped me to stop beating myself up about my dishonesty in failing to pursue my heart's desires.

I still had to "own" the issue, of course, because I could see how God had brought me to many places in my life where, if I had simply allowed myself to be humbled, I would have admitted to what I really wanted to do in life. It took being knocked flat on my back (as it does for most of us) before I was humbled enough to finally expose myself on these deeper levels.

I think an important point here is that no one can unknowingly live a lie forever, for at some point in life's journey, each person is brought to the awareness that he or she is being dishonest. Through the trials He provides, God *ensures* that such an awareness will occur. He ensures that what is in our hearts eventually rises to the surface through the circumstances that He orchestrates in our lives. He does this because He wants everything to be exposed to the light so that our hearts may be healed, and this healing will not happen if one is frozen in denial under a rigid, rule-governed structure. God's law is precisely such a rigid, rule-governed structure—one that keeps a person frozen in denial every bit as powerfully as the rules and regulations of any home environment.

Surely, we realize that the law has no healing power to restore our shattered hearts, nor does it have any nurturing power to nourish and strengthen the new creation in Christ. It has only judgmental power to condemn. Since the Bible is clear that there is no condemnation for God's children (Romans 8:1), it is likewise clear that all who have been born again in Christ have died to the law.

- "So, my brothers and sisters, you also died to the law through the body of Christ, that you might belong to another, to him who was raised from the dead, in order that we might bear fruit for God" (Romans 7:4).
- "For through the law I died to the law so that I might live for God. I have been crucified with Christ and I no longer live, but Christ lives in me" (Galatians 2:19, 20).

Ask yourself the following questions:

- Why would a child of God need an external, impersonal constraint like the law?
- Does such a born-again believer really need to be told through specific commandments that he or she shouldn't lie, steal, murder or commit adultery?
- Do we not experience the tender voice of the Holy Spirit when we think or act in a manner that brings pain to our Father's heart?

As I stated at the beginning of this chapter, the law provides an ongoing source of objective guidance for the ignorant and the wayward. So, for example, the fourth commandment could inform someone who had never known about the institution of God's Sabbath. I am not now concerned, however, with those who are unknowingly ignorant of some aspect of God's law, nor am I concerned about those who are deliberately wayward. Rather, I am concerned about those who genuinely desire to grow in grace, and if there is one truth that all of us need to know, it is this: A focus on the law will greatly retard anyone's growth in grace because such a focus will keep one in bondage and denial. God's Word speaks of this repeatedly, so we must not allow ourselves to be blind to this reality. We must not allow ourselves to improperly interpret a few statements of Scripture to believe that we should be setting our minds to keeping God's law.

Consider how Paul describes his fellow Israelites when writing to the Corinthians:

"But their minds were made dull, for to this day the same veil remains when the old covenant is read. It has not been removed, because only in Christ is it taken away. Even to this day when Moses is read, a veil covers their hearts. But whenever anyone turns to the Lord, the veil is taken away. Now the Lord is the Spirit, and where the Spirit of the Lord is, there is freedom" (2 Corinthians 3:14–17).

Paul is describing the "veil over the understanding"[15] that existed in the hearts and minds of the unbelieving Jews when they read the law. He mentions that, when one turns to the Lord, this veil is taken away because the Lord is the Spirit, and the Spirit brings—not denial and bondage—but, rather, honesty and freedom.

I do not mean to imply that sin, that is, the breaking of God's law (1 John 3:4), is not serious before God because we know that it is. Furthermore, I think that we all realize that God is often addressing this very issue of sin in our lives through the agency of trials. Nevertheless, if we set our minds to keeping God's law when we are persevering through difficult times, then we simply bind ourselves to bondage and denial. Indeed, any attempt to deal with the issues of our hearts with a set of cold, impersonal standards like God's commandments—during a trial or any other time—will never bring healing and restoration.

Consider a simple example: Imagine that all of us are going through difficult times, and we are coping by eating significant quantities of potato chips, chocolate chip cookies, and ice cream. The effect of this indulgence is that we are slowly killing ourselves, and we know that killing ourselves is against God's law, for it is in direct violation of the sixth commandment that states, "Thou shalt not kill." Furthermore, we are polluting the temple of the Holy Spirit.

So, suppose we take drastic measures to ensure that we no longer eat potato chips, chocolate chip cookies, and ice cream—we hire someone to handle all our money and do all our food shopping for us. In this way, we never have money available to buy our pet indulgences. What would this approach accomplish for us? Would it not keep us in denial of the real issues in our hearts that lead to such law-breaking and temple-destroying behavior? And would it not put us in a position where we would soon find ourselves dealing with yet *another* lawbreaking and temple-destroying behavior because we have not yet dealt with the underlying issues in the first?

---

15 This is a phrase used by J. F. Strombeck in his work, *Shall Never Perish: Eternal Security Examined* (Moline, IL: Strombeck Agency, Inc., 1956, 8th ed.), p. 165.

What *are* the underlying issues that each of us must address in our frequent junk food indulgences? What feelings are we trying to stuff with this behavior? Are we lonely? Is there a pocket of emptiness in our lives? Do we have an uncomfortable sense that our existence is devoid of meaning and purpose? Are we filled with remorse or bitterness or anger or fear or insecurity or a hundred other feelings that we are currently incapable of facing honestly?

These are the levels at which the problem must be addressed, and these are the levels at which God will address the problem through the agency of the Holy Spirit. But we must allow everything to "bubble up." We cannot allow the true issues of our hearts to be stuffed by a robotic adherence to the cold, external demands of God's impersonal, heartless commandments. A rigid adherence to God's commandments can keep someone in denial just as powerfully as anything else, and we are especially prone to find "refuge" in the defensive structure of such a rigid adherence during times of trial when we are weak and vulnerable.

Suppose, for example, that God brings a weight upon my spirit to lead me to become active in a specific ministry, to help a person in need, or to humble myself by confessing a wrong to someone. Suppose I respond by saying, "I'm not going to do that. I'm going to get drunk instead." Alcohol can certainly keep me in denial, right? I can stuff my feelings by getting drunk; thus, I can remain "comfortably" deceived about my nature and my behavior.

But what if I respond to this quickening of my spirit in a different way? What if I say, "I'm not going to do that. I'm too busy over here keeping God's commandments and doing all this religious stuff." I can safely assure you that this supposed obedience to God's law (along with a measure of religious busyness) will keep me in denial every bit as powerfully as alcohol, drugs, gambling, sex, or anything else.

If you still have doubt about how a robotic adherence to the law can keep someone in denial, then simply consider the law-and-commandment-focused Pharisees. How delusional can a people be? They witnessed the truth and power of Christ's words, the miracles of healing, the raising of Lazarus from the dead, yet they were unfazed. They went to arrest the "imposter," and Jesus instantly restored a man's ear that had been cut off by Peter. Again, they were unfazed. They just wanted the "imposter" to be bound, beaten, and crucified, and all the while they saw themselves as the law-keeping, obedient people of God.

Now *that's* delusion! But, truly, God's law can keep people in the deepest delusion.

If anyone responds to what I have written by saying, "Stuart Cedrone thinks God's commandments have been abolished; he believes we can lie, cheat, steal, and commit adultery"—well, I will deny it. Clearly, this is not the point I am making at all, and anyone who reads my words in an unbiased way will understand this. God's grace in Christ has always produced a people who reverence the principles of God's law, and His people will surely be known for their purity of heart and life.

My point is simply this: Those who are saved by God's grace are never focused or aware of how they are "measuring up" as "perfect keepers of God's commandments." Rather, they invariably have a deep sense of their unworthiness as well as a deep sense of their need—their utter need—of God's mercy. Even the great apostle Paul states, "Here is a trustworthy saying that deserves full acceptance: Christ Jesus came into the world to save sinners—of whom I am the worst" (1 Timothy 1:15).

> *God's grace in Christ has always produced a people who reverence the principles of God's law, and His people will surely be known for their purity of heart and life.*

All of us should have this sense of sinful unworthiness, for we have witnessed firsthand how God has loved and accepted us even after He has seen into the depths of our wretched and polluted hearts. Furthermore, we should experience an intensified awareness of our sinfulness and unworthiness as we grow in His grace because, as we grow closer to God, we see more and more clearly the true nature of ourselves in relation to His purity and holiness.

"The closer we get, the farther away we seem."

Have you ever had the experience of thinking you're dutifully doing something important as an obedient and law-keeping believer, and then, suddenly, God overwhelms you with His presence in a way that allows you to see how empty of life and power your works really are? I mentioned the time when God overwhelmed me with His presence for hours when I was in the throes of a deep depression, but there have been other (shorter) experiences like this as well. Whenever I have experiences like these, I always find myself thinking, *So that's what God is like!* In other words, the overflowing fullness of God's love and tenderness makes me realize how pure and loving and perfect our God is. This overflowing fullness of God's love and tenderness should be the motivation for all the works in our lives—but, of course, it isn't. The fact that it isn't is the principal reason that we should always be in a repentant mode of confession before the Father. In other words, only the fullness of the Spirit's presence has power to change lives. Our empty words and works surely don't. Therefore, we should always be in a repentant mode where we are confessing our desperate need of the life and power of the Holy Spirit.

I hope we do not allow ourselves to fall into the trap of living "old covenant" lives of dutiful service when God desires that we live "new covenant" lives of joyful freedom in the Spirit. Everything in relation to keeping God's commandments will eventually flow from these new covenant lives in the Spirit.

In summary, times of trial are times of healing and restoration; therefore, they should be times of spiritual rest. As we are healed and restored during these times of trial, we will have no sense of being dutiful and obedient "commandment keepers." Rather, like the twenty-four elders before God's throne, we will spontaneously cast our crowns at God's feet (Revelation 4:10), knowing that He alone has done all the work in our lives.

We should be careful, however, not to rush things, especially during the trying times of our lives. We must be patient with ourselves in our paths of growth, remembering that "a little leaven leavens the whole lump [eventually!]" (Galatians 5:9, NKJV). I will address this important topic of "leavening" (that is, spiritual growth) more directly in the next two chapters.

* * *

Praise God from whom all blessings flow.

Chapter 8
We Are Growing in Christ, Part 1

"But grow in the grace and knowledge of our Lord and Savior Jesus Christ."

(2 Peter 3:18)

    I have written considerably in the previous two chapters about how our growth becomes stagnated when we focus upon keeping external, impersonal standards like God's law. In the present chapter, I will explain the nature of true growth in grace as we abide in Christ.

    Growth in the Christian life is certainly important, and we who take our spiritual lives seriously should not expect to remain the same babes in Christ as the months and the years pass by. We should not continue to feed on spiritual milk, nor should we continue to be attracted to the things of this world. On the contrary, we should expect a continually progressing maturity that leads to a diet of spiritual meat as well as an earthly life that reveals an increasing devotion and consecration to our Savior.

    The reality, however, is often quite different than this. Many Christians become less rather than more intense in their devotion to our Savior as the months and the years pass by. The fervency and the zeal of the initial conversion experience slowly ebb away, and these believers become more worldly and accommodating. One cannot help but ask, "Why is this?"

    Before addressing the answer, I will state that when we, as God's children, lose the fervency and zeal of our initial conversion experience, we can almost certainly expect a crisis of some kind to intrude upon our worldly, accommodating lives. This is so because crises are often the only ways to get our attention. God jolts us through an extremity to break us from our worldly satisfaction and to drive us to seek the comfort that only He can provide. If we learn the key to growth in grace, we will thus spare ourselves many of these trying times that God uses to draw us back to the fold of the Good Shepherd.

Hannah Smith, a nineteenth-century Quaker woman, addressed this issue of spiritual growth in her well-known book, *The Christian's Secret of a Happy Life*.[16] She believed that Christians fail to grow in grace because they are not thoroughly planted in the unconditional love of the Father for His children in Christ.

Smith initially points out that the standard definition given for grace is the "free unmerited favor" of God. You have doubtless heard this definition many times. She states that this definition of grace expresses only "a little of its meaning." She believes that the reality of grace in the life of the believer has a substance and a fullness that this expression fails to capture. In her words, grace in the life of the believer is a realization as well as an experience of the "unhindered, wondrous, boundless love of God, poured out upon us in an infinite variety of ways, without stint or measure, not according to our deserving, but according to His measureless heart of love."[17]

This is certainly true, for the biblical message of salvation is clearly this: Believers are freely forgiven for Christ's sake, and God treats them as the perfect Man, Jesus Himself, deserves to be treated. Therefore, since grace in the life of the believer is the realization and experience of this "unhindered, wondrous, boundless love of God," we need to grow in our understanding and awareness of *this love* if we would grow *at all* in the Christian life. We must "be planted in the very heart of this Divine love, be enveloped by it, steeped in it" if we wish to experience the continually progressing maturity of one who is growing in grace.

Hannah Smith summarizes the matter in this way: "… the soul … must let itself out to the joy of it [that is, the "unhindered, wondrous, boundless love of God"], and must refuse to know anything else. It must grow in the apprehension of it day by day, and it must intrust everything to its care, and must have no shadow of doubt but that it will surely order all things well."[18]

---

16 Hannah Whitall Smith, *The Christian's Secret of a Happy Life*.
17 Smith, p. 174.
18 Smith, p. 175.

Personally, I have never read a better practical description of a grace-filled life.

I will emphasize again that, if the grace of God is the "unhindered, wondrous, boundless love of God" poured out upon forgiven sinners in an "infinite variety of ways," and it surely is, we must grow in our understanding and experience of *this love* if we would grow *at all* in the Christian life.

The unfortunate reality, however, is that we often stray from a genuine experience of this love that God pours into our hearts through the Holy Spirit (Romans 5:5). This is especially true when we become legalistic Christians who place an unbalanced emphasis upon God's commandments rather than upon His tenderness and compassion. While in this condition, we often overlook the fact that the true substance and reality of the Christian life is an authentic *experience* with God, a bona fide *communion* with the Father and the Son through the agency of the Holy Spirit. As the apostle John wrote: "Our fellowship is with the Father and with his Son, Jesus Christ" (1 John 1:3). And again: "This is how we know that we live in him and he in us: He has given us of His own Spirit" (1 John 4:13).

If we do not experience this communion with the Father and the Son that the Bible describes, then, clearly, something is wrong. Since God's Word promises this experience to honest believers in Christ, the problem for those of us who do not enjoy this spiritual communion would have to be *dis*honesty on some level. In other words, if we do not experience communion with the Father and the Son, then we are not being honest with ourselves or with God.

> *If we do not experience this communion with the Father and the Son that the Bible describes, then, clearly, something is wrong.*

We see this in the lives of Adam and Eve after they sinned in the Garden of Eden. They would not admit that they had done wrong. They would not be honest with themselves, nor would they be honest with God. Each brought forth a convenient excuse rather than a straightforward confession, and this allowed each to remain conveniently in denial. Since we are sons and daughters of the fallen Adam and the fallen Eve, we can be assured that this dishonesty with ourselves and with God comes quite naturally to us, as it did to them.

But God understands this. He understands that our natural tendency is toward self-protecting defense mechanisms like projection and denial. He knows that we would rather play the "blame game" than expose ourselves through any honest vulnerability. For this reason, He mercifully allows difficult times to come upon us, and the adversity of these situations causes the true issues of our hearts to rise to the surface. In this way, each of us can be brought to the point of awareness, confession, and ultimate healing.

Until this process of healing is brought to completion, however, we will be typical works-oriented believers who lack the sweet awareness of full acceptance in Christ. We will thus be living "Christian" lives where we are forever attempting to secure personal merit before God. In short, we will be attempting to grow *into* grace rather than *in* it. Hannah Smith writes about such individuals as follows:

> They are like a rosebush, planted by a gardener in the hard, stony path, with a view to its growing *into* the flower-bed and which has of course dwindled and withered in consequence, instead of flourishing and maturing. The children of Israel, wandering in the wilderness, are a perfect picture of this sort of growing. They were travelling about for forty years, taking many weary steps, and finding but little rest from their wanderings; and yet, at the end of it all, were no nearer the promised land than they were at the beginning. . . . All their wanderings and fightings in the wilderness had not put them in possession of one inch of the promised land. In order to get possession of this land, it was necessary first to be in it; and in order to grow in grace, it is necessary first to be planted in grace. When once in the land, however, their conquest was rapid; and when once planted in grace, the growth of the spiritual life becomes vigorous and rapid beyond all conceiving. For grace is a most fruitful soil, and the plants that grow therein are plants of a marvelous growth. They are tended by a Divine Husbandman, and are warmed by the Sun of Righteousness, and watered by the dew from Heaven. Surely, it is no wonder that they bring forth fruit "some an hundred-fold, some sixty-fold, some thirty-fold."[19]

Whenever we slip into the "dwindled and withered" state of which Hannah Smith writes, it is important to realize that true healing and res-

---
19 Smith, pp. 173, 174.

toration is only a confession of need away. A flood of living, healing water will begin to flow into our withered hearts once we simply confess—in an honest way—our desperate need of God's mercy.

Whenever we are languishing on a "hard, stony path," we should never seek to remedy this "dwindled and withered" state by seeking approval from God through acts of dutiful service. We should not look to ourselves for deservedness through acts of supposed obedience, for, in so doing, we will fail to receive all that God seeks to bestow upon us through the merit of His Son. Truly, the remedy for any deficiency or lack of growth in our lives is always found in the life of our Savior—never in us. So, again, we need only confess our great need.

If God brings something to our awareness when we are confessing our need to Him, then we must, of course, take this very seriously. He might, for example, cause us to remember a person whom we have wronged. In such a case, we need to realize that He is calling us to confess to the person and possibly to make restitution as well.

All of this is simply part of the process by which God sanctifies His children, and we should not be alarmed or troubled by it. An increasing awareness of past wrongdoing during times of confession to God is not a sign that we are being condemned, for the Bible is clear that there is "no condemnation for those who are in Christ Jesus" (Romans 8:1). Rather, it is a sign that God is gently leading us as His children in a path of honesty and purity. We should expect nothing less than this from our heavenly Father, and we can rest assured that His presence will be with us through the entire process.

Do not allow yourself to be overwhelmed by this process to the point that you despair of ever reaching the other side. Your Father in heaven is faithful, and He will provide all the needed grace and strength for you. He will also provide any material blessings needed to make things right with others. "Fret not yourself; it tends only to evil" (Psalm 37:8, RSV).

A further point in this area of growth is that all true growth in grace is quite the opposite of growth in self-dependence or self-effort. "Which of you by taking thought can add one cubit unto his stature?" (Matthew 6:27, KJV) And again, "See how the flowers of the field grow. They do not labor or spin" (Matthew 6:28). As Hannah Smith rightly concludes, if our experience is one of "toiling and spinning" for ourselves great spiritual garments, or one of "stretching and straining" in our efforts toward spiritual growth, we can be sure that we are "growing backward rather than forward."[20]

> *Upon God's Will I lay me down,*
> *As child upon its mother's breast;*
> *No silken couch, nor softest bed,*
> *Could ever give me such sweet rest.*[21]

Do we abide in this place of comfort and rest? If not, then it is because we are not planted in the blessed grace of God; therefore, we are not growing.

Another important point is that all growth in grace is a growth in one's realization of how God's favor is *un*merited. This is grace. Thus, if we are truly *growing* in grace, there will be a deepening of repentance, a greater sense of need and dependence. Jesus will become all and in all, and He will be our *only* hope of salvation. Those who are growing in grace would never think of themselves as *more* able to keep God's commandments; rather, they will see God's immutable law as the perfect, holy standard that it is and will realize that it is as far above them as the stars. They will not think of themselves as stronger but will realize more and more how utterly weak and dependent upon the Savior they truly are.

Growth in grace is a growth in the *faith* that allows us to claim more and still more of the boundless riches that we know we do not deserve. Those who are growing in grace can claim these riches because they reach the point in their lives that they see how fully Jesus deserves those riches. They are then able to claim them confidently in Jesus' name because they experience sweet communion with the Father and the Son, and this allows them to realize how completely God accepts them for the sake of their Savior.

Since growth in the Christian life is a growth in our realization and experience of God's boundless love for us in Christ, we must be careful to understand and appreciate this love for what it truly is. We must not, for example, allow ourselves to believe any lies of the devil that distort and degrade this love into something it is not. Consider what Hannah Smith writes about God's love:

---

20 Smith, p. 177.
21 Madam Guyon, quoted by Smith, p. 154.

I sometimes think that a totally different meaning is given to the word "love" when it is associated with God, from that which we so well understand in its human application. We seem to consider that Divine love is hard and self-seeking and distant, concerned about its own glory, and indifferent to the fate of others. But if ever human love was tender and self-sacrificing and devoted, if ever it could bear and forbear, if ever it could suffer gladly for its loved one, if ever it was willing to pour itself out in lavish abandonment for the comfort or pleasure of its objects then infinitely more is Divine love tender and self-sacrificing and devoted, and glad to bear and to forbear, and suffer, and eager to lavish its best of gifts and blessings upon the objects of its love. Put together all the tenderest love you know of, dear reader, the deepest you have ever felt, and the strongest that has ever been poured out upon you, and heap upon it all the love of all the loving human hearts in the world, and then multiply it by infinity, and you will begin perhaps to have some faint glimpses of the love and grace of God![22]

One can hardly read such words without being brought to tears! I hope all of us have experienced this loving tenderness of God as described in these words. I have certainly experienced it myself—especially during the times in my life when I needed this care the most.

Consider two further descriptions of God's love:

All the paternal love which has come down from generation to generation through the channel of human hearts, all the springs of tenderness which have opened in the souls of men, are but as a tiny rill to the boundless ocean when compared with the infinite, exhaustless love of God. Tongue cannot utter it; pen cannot portray it. You may meditate upon it every day of your life; you may search the Scriptures diligently in order to understand it; you may summon every power and capability that God has given you, in the endeavor to comprehend the love and compassion of the heavenly Father; and yet there is an infinity beyond. You may study that love for ages; yet you can never fully comprehend the length and the

---

22   Smith, pp. 174, 175.

breadth, the depth and the height, of the love of God in giving His Son to die for the world. Eternity itself can never fully reveal it.[23]

The gift of Christ reveals the Father's heart. It testifies that the thoughts of God toward us are "thoughts of peace and not of evil." Jeremiah 29:11. It declares that while God's hatred of sin is as strong as death, His love for the sinner is stronger than death. Having undertaken our redemption, He will spare nothing, however dear, which is necessary to the completion of His work. No truth essential to our salvation is withheld, no miracle of mercy is neglected, no divine agency is left unemployed. Favor is heaped upon favor, gift upon gift. The whole treasury of heaven is open to those He seeks to save. Having collected the riches of the universe, and laid open the resources of infinite power, He gives them all into the hands of Christ, and says, All these are for man. Use these gifts to convince him that there is no love greater than Mine in earth or heaven. His greatest happiness will be found in loving Me."[24]

So, can you and I say that we are at least *beginning* to understand the height and depth of God's love? I hope so, for nothing will stimulate our growth in Christ more than a correct understanding and a true appreciation of this. Likewise, nothing will hinder our growth more than an incorrect understanding or a lack of appreciation of it.

The central point that we must understand is a simple one: Our God *really is* a God of infinite love who seeks to pour out the blessings of omnipotence upon us. Furthermore, He is a God of infinite wisdom who always knows what is best for us. We must therefore simply admit our great need of His mercy and then claim the fullness of His gift to us in Christ. These two simple acts, admitting our need and claiming Christ's fullness, will, by God's own providence, lead to a life of joyous uplifting and heartfelt obedience.

I hope we always remember that the key to spiritual growth is being planted in the assurance of God's love and favor toward us in Christ and that the means to being planted here is simple honesty regarding our personal need and dependence. It is especially important to be honest about our state of need and dependence during the crises of our lives because we

---

23 Ellen G. White, *Testimonies for the Church*, vol. 5 (Boise, Idaho: Pacific Press Publishing Association, 1948), p. 740.
24 Ellen G. White, *The Desire of Ages* (https://1ref.us/zg, accessed February 10, 2020), p. 57.

are often prone during these times to try to "prove" ourselves to God. In short, we are prone to try to grow *into* grace rather than to grow *in* it. But growing *in* grace is the key, and this growth will eventually lead us to claim as our own the fullness of God's "indescribable gift" (2 Corinthians 9:15).

> For no matter how many promises God has made, they are "Yes" in Christ. And so through him the "Amen" is spoken by us to the glory of God. (2 Corinthians 1:20)

* * *

Praise God from whom all blessings flow.

Chapter 9
We Are Growing in Christ, Part 2

> *"But the fruit of the Spirit is love, joy, peace,*
> *Forbearance, kindness, goodness,*
> *Faithfulness, gentleness, self-control;*
> *Against such things there is no law."*
>
> *(Galatians 5:22, 23)*

I emphasized in the previous chapter that the key to growth is to confess our dependency to God and to allow ourselves to be firmly planted in His grace—and then to rest there. As we rest in Christ, we grow in grace, and our lives invariably bring forth fruit.

I think we are all familiar with the fruit of the Spirit that Paul mentions in the verses above, but there is a fruit of Christian growth that I personally believe is God's greatest gift of all, namely, deliverance from the projection and denial that normally accompany our fallen human condition. As I pointed out in an earlier chapter, we see this projection and denial in the experience of Adam and Eve in the Garden of Eden, and we see the same state of self-deception in our own experiences as well. We are encumbered with a dishonest tendency to refuse to take responsibility for our lives and, instead, to blame our problems on circumstances, on other people, and even on God Himself. "A person's own folly leads to their ruin, yet their heart rages against the Lord" (Proverbs 19:3).

I hope all of us can honestly acknowledge the many times our hearts have raged against the Lord even though it was our own folly that led us to ruin. Personally, I can't begin to tell you how many times I have felt anger in my heart against our merciful heavenly Father after I brought difficulty upon myself. It is a reflexive impulse that comes quite naturally to us in our fallen state, and it amazes me that God tolerates such behavior from us repeatedly.

Sometimes it has taken me years to arrive at a place where, by God's grace, I can finally say, "Oh, I see that was my fault." When I finally reach this place of enlightenment, I can discern the many ways that God tried to *protect* me from ruin rather than to lead me to it.

When God accomplishes a progressive deliverance from our natural tendency toward projection and denial, we are then free to experience Him as He truly is. It is this experience of God as He truly is that constitutes the very substance of salvation: "Now this is eternal life: that they know you, the only true God, and Jesus Christ, whom you have sent" (John 17:3).

In order to understand how our tendency toward projection and denial affects our perception and experience of God, consider the parable of the talents in Matthew 25. Here we encounter a servant who was given a bag of gold. This servant then "went off, dug a hole in the ground and hid his master's money" (Matthew 25:18). When his master returned to settle accounts, the servant stated, "Master, ... I knew that you are a hard man, harvesting where you have not sown and gathering where you have not scattered seed. So I was afraid and went out and hid your gold in the ground. See, here is what belongs to you" (Matthew 25:24, 25).

How did this servant "know" that his master was a hard man, and how did he "know" that his master harvested where he did not sow and gathered where he had not scattered seed? Clearly, the master represents God. Is God a "hard man"? Does He harvest where He does not sow and gather where He has not scattered seed? This servant is thinking of God in the same manner that Adam and Eve did after they had fallen. They ran and hid from Him, so, they, too, obviously thought of Him as a "hard man."

Surely, we know that God is not a "hard man." Yet, the servant in the parable—as well as the fallen Adam and the fallen Eve, who accurately represent you and me—are prone to think of God in this way. Why is that?

Consider what God's word says of Him in Psalm 18: "To the faithful you show yourself faithful, to the blameless you show yourself blameless, to the pure you show yourself pure, but to the devious you show yourself shrewd" (Psalm 18:25, 26). You will see these same verses in 2 Samuel 22:26, 27.

What is going on here? Is God playing a clever game with people? Why does He show Himself faithful to those who are faithful and shrewd to those who are devious? Is He putting on a faithful mask for the faithful people and a shrewd mask for the devious people?

Consider what God says in Psalm 50: "You thought I was exactly like you" (Psalm 50:21). Now everything becomes clear. We see from this text in the Psalms that God is not playing a clever game. He has no need to put on different masks for different people, because each person cannot help but perceive God in a way that harmonizes with his or her own experience. This is why people say, "It takes one to know one."

If I am a contriving person, for example, then of course I will experience you as being contriving. You may be a kind person who is simply trying to do something nice for me, but I will experience you as someone who has something "up your sleeve" because I do not know what it is to be pure in heart and ingenuous. These qualities simply do not compute for me; therefore, I do not experience anyone in this way. I experience everyone as contriving like me because this is the only state of being that I know (unless God provides deliverance).

The important point is this: We project our "stuff" (our qualities) onto others, and we project it onto God as well. The servant experienced his master as a "hard man" because *he* was a hard man. He experienced his master as someone who "harvested where he did not sow" because *he* was someone who harvested where he did not sow.

Notice that, in the parable, the master does not argue with the servant. He does not defend himself against false charges. Rather, he simply applies the servant's own principle to the servant's situation: "You wicked, lazy servant! So you knew that I harvest where I have not sown and gather where I have not scattered seed? Well then, you should have put my money on deposit with the bankers, so that when I returned I would have received it back with interest" (Matthew 25:26, 27).

God responds this way in our lives as well. When we project our "stuff" onto God and think of Him as one "exactly like" ourselves (Psalm 50:21), He does not argue with us. He does not defend Himself against false charges. Rather, He simply applies the principles embedded in our projections to our personal situation, and He relates to us in this manner. As He states in His Word: "For in the same way you judge others, you will be judged, and with the measure you use, it will be measured to you" (Matthew 7:2).

The central point of the parable is that simply getting what we give and being judged by the principles of our own judgment—this alone is enough to drive us to confess our need of a Savior. Whether we do, in fact, confess this need depends upon whether we are honest enough to face the truth of our situation rather than become further entrenched in denial. This is where we must be careful during the trials of our lives. We must be careful to do the one thing that we *can* do—namely, confess the truth. We may be weaker than weak and thus see no hope for ourselves, but we should not allow this sense of hopelessness to cause us to lie to ourselves, to others, or to God.

When life is catching up with us, when our deeds are returning on our own heads, when the "measure" we have used is being "measured" back to us—let us cry out to God for deliverance rather than "wail upon our beds" (Hosea 7:14). Let us place honest trust in the Unfailing One rather than find deceptive "refuge" in lies, excuses, and blame. If we place honest trust in God by accepting the Savior that He has freely given, then we will get—not the little we have chosen to give—but, rather, the abundance we have refused to give. We will be judged—not by the hard, legalistic principles of our own judgment—but, rather, by the soft, loving principles of God's mercy.

This experience breaks our hard, legalistic hearts and makes them soft and pliable in our Father's hands. This happens because we learn firsthand that—although the law demands that we love our God with all our hearts, souls, and minds (Deuteronomy 6:5), and we have failed miserably in doing this—yet, God still pours His grace into our sin-polluted hearts and reveals that, "This is love: not that we loved God, but that he loved us and sent his Son as an atoning sacrifice for our sins" (1 John 4:10).

Have you ever been involved in the simplest task, and, then, suddenly, your heart breaks as the Holy Spirit associates something in your activity with God's mercy toward you? I experience this sort of occurrence often, and it always causes me to experience a deep emotional catharsis as well as a spiritual release. My heart rises in thanksgiving to God for His great tenderness and love, and I invariably weep.

I hope you experience such times as well. For me, life would be dead and lifeless without them. These are the times when God enlivens and softens my spirit with His fullness. He pours His uncreated life into my thirsty soul, and I experience in an authentic spiritual way His tender heart of compassion and love. Christ truly becomes all and in all during the ensuing catharsis and release, and the life of our merciful Father suddenly fills every aspect of my awareness. Experiences like these open my eyes to see the many tokens of God's love and care, and I always find myself overwhelmed.

This, I would say, is what it means to be broken. This is what it means to have the wall of projection and denial come crashing down in our lives so that we no longer consider our Father in heaven to be a "hard man." I will state it again: When we are delivered from all the lies, excuses, and blame in our lives, then God is able to reveal Himself to us as He truly is, and this is the greatest revelation of all.

> *When we are delivered from all the lies, excuses, and blame in our lives, then God is able to reveal Himself to us as He truly is.*

For me, these experiences of God's fullness often occur at the strangest times—times when I am least expecting them. I think God orchestrates this "strangeness" intentionally so I will know that the experiences are solely a gift of His grace and not the result of any spiritual "heart preparation" on my part during times of Bible study or worship. I do not mean to imply that times of Bible study and worship are not important, for they surely are. But these times will do nothing to soften our hearts if we are not fit vessels to receive the tender influence of the Holy Spirit.

I often experience these times of God's fullness when I am enjoying a time of personal relaxation. I might be watching a movie, for example, and someone in the movie will perform a courageous and heroic act. I immediately become quite emotional because God reveals to me that the only true hero is Christ Himself, and He also reveals His great mercy toward me for the sake of His Son's heroism. My heart is lifted to Him in gratitude, and I am brought to tears.

I honestly think that, if we always had a true awareness of God, we would be crying out to Him continuously in tearful words of gratitude and praise. How could we not be doing this if we have a true awareness of His great mercy and glory?

I should mention that even though I am explaining this experience in many words, when the experience occurs, it happens in an instant. It is a spontaneous spiritual awareness of the greatness and majesty of God as well as an awareness of His mercy—His great, great mercy—toward a poor, wretched sinner like me.

One final point about growth: A little leaven truly does leaven the whole lump (Galatians 5:9). Since God's Word states this truth, we should not become impatient as we seek to grow in grace. We should not expect that God will instantly remove all the devil's strongholds in our lives when we come to Christ.

When the children of Israel were about to enter the Promised Land, God said to them, "The Lord your God will clear away these nations before you little by little; you may not make an end of them at once, lest the wild beasts grow too numerous for you" (Deuteronomy 7:22).

The heathen nations during this time represent the devil's strongholds in our lives, yet God made it clear to His people that He would remove these nations "little by little." And why would He remove them little by little? God Himself states the reason: To ensure that the wild beasts do not grow too numerous.

Clearly, there were other dangers on the geographical landscape of which the Israelites were unaware, and if God were to make a quick end of the resident heathen nations, then these other dangers (namely, the wild beasts) would cause great problems for His people. Likewise, there are other dangers on our "geographical landscapes" besides the ones of which we may be aware. For this reason, we should not think we are failing to grow in grace because all Satan's strongholds do not instantly disappear for us at conversion. God is growing us in ways that are consistent with His perfect principles of harmony and balance, and we will often learn many important lessons through failure.

If we become impatient with God's working in our lives, then we will invariably endeavor to implement some sort of "sanctification by works" to get our lives "swept clean and put in order" (Matthew 12:44). We will begin to make self-conscious efforts to be better rather than allowing ourselves to rest in the finished work of Christ so that we can experience the peace and inspiration of the Holy Spirit. When we embark on this course of action, we will soon find that the evil spirit that once plagued us will return with seven spirits "more wicked than itself," and our last state will be "worse than the first" (Matthew 12:45).

Surely, we can trust our heavenly Father with our lives and our growth. He knows what He is doing, and He knows our hearts. It often takes many hard lessons of failure before the truth of God's Word can enter a broken vessel.

A little of God's leaven truly does leaven the whole lump (Galatians 5:9). We simply need to give our wise and loving heavenly Father a bit of time.

* * *

Praise God from whom all blessings flow.

Chapter 10
We Are Born Again in Christ

> *Very truly I tell you, no one can see the kingdom of God*
> *Unless they are born again.*
>
> (John 3:3)

There are few topics of greater importance than the new birth, for nothing will help any of us in the path of salvation if we are not—at some point—born again. Our first birth in Adam leads only to death; thus, it is only the second—or new—birth that leads to life eternal.

Clearly, it would make more sense to cover this topic in a book on fundamental Christian doctrine rather than in one relating to empowerment for hard times. I have chosen to cover the topic in the present work, however, because it is central to every area of our Christian lives, and we become acutely aware of its centrality during seemingly hopeless situations.

Often, when I was enduring crisis situations, I was tormented with doubt about my status as a son of God in Christ. I would ask myself, "Am I *really* born again? Am I *really* a part of the family of God?" Doubts and questions such as these are better resolved before we find ourselves amid trying circumstances, for our thinking can be muddied and our emotional state fragile during such times.

I am happy to say that I am no longer tormented by such questions or doubts during the trying times of my life. I now find rest during these difficult periods, knowing that my heavenly Father is accomplishing a needed work in my life. Before I understood the true nature and effects of a believer's new birth, however, I could find no rest during these periods because I never knew with certainty that I was a part of the family of God. I often wondered if I were not being justly punished as a rebellious unbeliever rather than lovingly disciplined as an adopted child.

Another reason to cover this topic in a book about points of grace related to trying times is that it often takes a crisis to knock us flat on our backs so that we finally look up. This is because the desire to live lives independently of God's direction goes deeply in all of us—to our very core. We just flat out want to be in control of our lives. Therefore, it often takes a time of severe extremity to break this foothold and bring us to the point of seeing our deep need of higher wisdom and guidance. This awareness culminates when we see our desperate need of full redemption, and we cry out to God for salvation. If we do this with honest hearts that place their full faith in Christ as Savior, then it is at this point that we are born again.

The third chapter of John's Gospel explains the importance and centrality of the new birth. Indeed, the verse quoted at the beginning of this chapter leaves no room for compromise or ambiguity, for it states plainly that, if we are not born again, we cannot even see the kingdom of God. The effect of this new birth is as follows:

- It ushers us into the fellowship of the Father and the Son (1 John 1:3).

- It allows us to "taste and see that the Lord is good" (Psalm 34:8).

- It opens the floodgates to the living water that becomes in us a well of water springing up into everlasting life (John 4:14).

Two Bible texts that I mentioned earlier are relevant here: (1) "Our fellowship is with the Father and with his Son, Jesus Christ" (1 John 1:3). (2) "This is how we know that we live in him and he in us: He has given us of his Spirit" (1 John 4:13). The Bible is thus clear that those who are born into the family of God experience spiritual communion with their heavenly Father. Therefore, the first question we must ask ourselves is this: Do we experience this spiritual communion with God? If we do not, then our condition is serious indeed, for God's desire for His children is that they confidently assert, "By God's grace I have been born again. I have been mercifully ushered into the Land of Promise, and I now enjoy fellowship with the Father and the Son." Surely this is what it means to be a part of the family of God.

If anyone is wondering *how* to be born again, the answer is simple: We confess to God that we are rebellious sinners in desperate need of redemption, and we place our faith in God's Son, Jesus Christ, as our Savior from sin. As simple as this sounds, however, it is precisely this act of confession that most rebellious sinners refuse to do. Those who are rigidly bound to the pride and sufficiency of this fallen world will not confess their need to God; therefore, they will not cry to Him for a savior: "They do not cry out to me from their hearts, but wail on their beds" (Hosea 7:14).

The proud and autonomous of this world (which is our natural state, of course) would rather wail upon their beds than cry out to God from their hearts. They would rather murmur and complain than confess their state of need. They would rather worry, and worry, and then worry some more than expose any honest vulnerability or need. In short, those who are bound to the pomp and pride of this fallen world would rather live autonomous lives of misery and pain than allow God to *be* God in their lives.

Let's assume for the moment that we are not like those who would rather wail upon their beds than cry out to God for deliverance. Let's further assume that we have confessed our desperate need to God and have accepted Christ as our Savior. (The Bible is clear that these are the only conditions we must fulfill for personal salvation—Acts 16:31; Romans 10:9.) How can we now have biblically based assurance that we are truly born again? We realize, of course, that we must take God's Word at face value without seeking a "sign" of our new birth on the level of feeling, for we walk by faith and not by sight (2 Corinthians 5:7). Nevertheless, we also realize that our hearts are "deceitful above all things" (Jeremiah 17:9), so we seek solid assurance that we are not deceiving ourselves.

With this understanding, I would say that each of us may obtain biblically based assurance of the new birth by simply answering four simple questions that are derived from the eighth chapter of the book of Romans since this chapter provides clear criteria for anyone to determine if he or she is born again in Christ.

Here are the four questions:

1. Do I experience the Spirit prompting me to cry, "Abba! Father!"—thus bearing witness with my spirit that I am a redeemed child of God? (Romans 8:15, 16).

2. Do I experience the Spirit prompting me to groan inwardly as I await the redemption of my body? (Romans 8:23).

3. Do I experience the Spirit interceding for me in prayer with "groanings which cannot be uttered"? (Romans 8:26, NKJV).

4. Do I experience God Himself searching my heart through the mind of the Spirit? (Romans 8:27).

Let's look at each of these questions more closely.

1. Do I experience the Spirit prompting me to cry, "Abba! Father!"?

Surely there is no substitute for this prompting of the Spirit, for how can we have a legitimate basis for believing that we are children of God if we do not experience this firsthand witness of the Holy Spirit that God is our Father and that we are His adopted children in Christ? Indeed, all of us, as God's children, need to know that we do indeed experience this prompting of the Holy Spirit causing us to cry out to God as our Father in Christ. This firsthand witness of the Holy Spirit that we are sons and daughters of the Most High is the first step in ushering us into deeper levels of intimacy with God as we grow in the grace and knowledge of our Savior (2 Peter 3:18). It also allows us to experience the peace and rest that flow from the spiritual release that accompanies this witness.

The unconverted of the world do not experience this personal testimony of the Holy Spirit because He has not taken permanent residence in their hearts. Those of the world experience only the Spirit's conviction of wrongdoing (which they suppress). They do not, however, experience His firsthand witness that God is their Father in Christ because they refuse to cry out for deliverance from sin. They likewise refuse to accept Jesus as their personal Savior.

Until a person is brought to the point of a desperate, wholehearted confession of need, he or she is entrenched in a posture of resistance. Therefore, every tender pleading of the Holy Spirit is stuffed or silenced.

2. Do I experience the Spirit prompting me to groan inwardly as I await the redemption of my body?

We who have been born again in Christ experience the peace and satisfaction that only God's uncreated life can provide. We therefore understand that no true or lasting fulfillment can result from abandoning ourselves to the impersonal, sensual impulses of the flesh. As we grow in God's grace, we yearn for more and still more of the peace and satisfaction that we experience from God's spiritual fullness, and this experience causes us to "groan inwardly" as we await the consummation of Christ's second coming. We "groan" because we know that this consummation will allow us to forever leave these bodies of sin and death that naturally lead to senseless, lustful pursuits.

As with the prior experience related to the new birth, the unconverted of the world know nothing of this inward groaning or yearning. They feel fully at home in their carnal bodies; therefore, they see no need to cry out for deliverance from the lust of the flesh, the lust of the eyes, and the pride of life (1 John 2:16). They yearn only for more opportunities to satisfy sensual cravings. They do not care that this is a senseless path of self-destruction leading to death (Romans 6:23)—for the unredeemed of the world *love* death (Proverbs 8:36).

3. Do I experience the Spirit interceding for me in prayer with "groanings which cannot be uttered"?

As children of the Most High, we experience times when God shares His heart burdens with us. During these times, our spirits are drawn out to Him in prayer, and we experience "groanings which cannot be uttered."

I can personally testify that the most intense spiritual "groanings" I have experienced occurred during times of adversity and trial. I have thus realized (finally!) that times of crisis and extremity truly are times of great blessing (James 1:2). During these times when our oft-hardened hearts are broken, we become far more sensitive to the tender promptings of a merciful and compassionate God. I can also testify to intense experiences of the Holy Spirit's intercession in the wee hours of the morning when the heavenly manna is falling. Lastly, I can testify to personal experiences of the Spirit's intercession when I have been totally self-absorbed and just doing my own thing.

I remember once when I was walking through Walmart, thinking about something I was going to purchase for my home. Suddenly God's Spirit broke through my self-absorption and drew my heart out to Him in such a powerful way that I began to weep. I remember spontaneously uttering the words, "I just want to love Jesus!"

Where did *that* prayer come from? Surely not from me. As I mentioned, I was just walking through Walmart, thinking about something I was going to purchase for my home. The prayer was from God, from the Spirit's intercession that broke through a heart that was *totally* self-absorbed.

4. Do I experience God searching my heart through the mind of the Spirit?

We who have been born again in Christ experience a spiritual witness that is constantly drawing our hearts to the truth as it is in Christ. This witness brings a dimension of honesty and authenticity to our lives that is found only among the children of God. This is the "searching of heart" through the "mind of the Spirit" of which the Bible speaks.

If you ever wondered why it is difficult to experience authentic interpersonal communication and connection with the unconverted of the world—well, this is why. The unconverted of the world have no abiding access to the mind of the Spirit, so they live in deep delusion. The truth that is so plain and evident to us is the result of the Spirit's "searching of heart" in God's children, but unbelievers have no access to this activity of the Spirit. Therefore, interpersonal truths and experiences that are easily accessible for us are, for them, on the other side of a wall of deep denial.

You will recall that I wrote of the "white elephant in the living room" in an earlier chapter. I mentioned that this is a phrase often used to refer to the atmosphere of projection and denial that engulfs dysfunctional families where one or more members are ensnared by addictive behavior. I also mentioned that there is a sense of awkwardness and tension in such families because the issues in their lives are not being faced with honesty; therefore, everyone is "out of touch" with no feeling of interpersonal connection.

My point here is that there is surely a "white elephant" in the life of each person who is living apart from Jesus because only He can enable a person to understand and face the issues of life honestly. All who are not children of the Most High cannot be real with you and with me because they refuse to be real with themselves and with God. It is only the "searching of heart" through the "mind of the Spirit" that draws an individual to truth, to a clear conscience, and to authentic connections with other people. Apart from this activity of the Spirit, people abide in delusion and disconnection.

Having examined the biblical criteria for determining if we are truly born again in Christ, we must now ask ourselves an obvious question: "What is one to do if he or she is currently enshrouded in darkness with no experience of the spiritual realities from Romans 8?

First, we need to understand that the solution to this problem is not to become self-absorbed by focusing inwardly on one's spiritual experience or lack of it, for this activity will help no one. What, then, is one to do? Simply this: Place a promise of God before Him and claim it in the name of Jesus, our Savior. I can assure you that our heavenly Father will respond—even during a time of spiritual deadness—and usher anyone with an honest heart into an experience of peace and rest. Truly, He has given us His Word on this.

I have found that Ezekiel 36:26, 27 contains powerful promises that one may claim during the bleakest times of darkness and despair. This is a well-known passage of Scripture, and it worked miraculously for me during one of the lowest points of my life: "I will give you a new heart and put a new spirit in you; I will remove from you your heart of stone and give you a heart of flesh. And I will put my Spirit in you and move you to follow my decrees and be careful to keep my laws" (Ezekiel 36:26, 27).

You can see that God has promised everything one would need in these verses. He has promised a new heart, and He has also promised to put His Own Spirit within us and to move us to obedience. I have found that deliverance from problematic times of darkness and despair results from simply claiming promises like these in the name of Jesus. One can then rest in the assurance of God's deliverance—regardless of the present nature of one's circumstances or experience.

I must emphasize that, although the new birth does indeed usher one into an actual experience with the Almighty, we should not expect to receive any confirmation of our new birth on the level of feeling because, again, we walk by faith and not by sight (2 Corinthians 5:7). The only confirmation we need is the Word of God, and we *have* this. So, we must simply accept as true that which we have every reason to accept as true, namely, the Word of the Living God.

The fact that our sinful hearts are hard and unspiritual does not change in the least what our heavenly Father has promised, and what He has promised is this: "I will give you a new heart, and I will put My Spirit within you." If we cling to this promise unflinchingly during times of sin, darkness, and despair, our heavenly Father will proceed to usher us into a rich experience with Himself, and we will soon feel His love and acceptance in real and affirming ways.

I can personally testify that I experienced this sort of deliverance myself during a time of seemingly hopeless darkness and despair. The deliverance came, not by any personal works or devotion on my part, but, rather, by simply resting in the promise that God has given to His children for the sake of His Son. It was a pure gift of grace given to an undeserving but forgiven sinner who simply confessed his need and trusted God.

If you are at a point in your experience where you believe you are unable to lay hold of this promise by faith, then confess this unbelief to God. Surely this is something you can do, so I would encourage you to do it. Just confess your unbelief to God and cry out for deliverance. You will find that your heavenly Father will meet you right where you are, as He always does, and He will strengthen your faith to claim all His fullness.

He did it for me. Trust Him to do it for you.

"This is how we know that He lives in us: we know it by the Spirit he gave us" (1 John 3:24).

* * *

Praise God from whom all blessings flow.

Chapter 11
Our Sinful Body Is Dead in Christ

*Don't you know that all of us who were baptized into Christ Jesus
Were baptized into his death?*

(Romans 6:3)

All of us are prone to doubt that our sinful bodies are dead in Christ, and the reason is obvious: We continue to struggle with various temptations, and we often commit sin when we fall under the power of these temptations. Nevertheless, despite our ongoing temptations and sinning, the Bible states clearly that our sinful bodies are dead in Christ.

How can this be?

Clarification about this matter can change one's entire understanding—as well as one's entire experience—of salvation in Christ. This change in understanding and experience will help tremendously during difficult times because it will keep us from lapsing into prolonged periods of self-doubt and self-hate. Let's begin by looking at some texts of Scripture:

- "For we know that our old self was crucified with him so that the body ruled by sin might be done away with, that we should no longer be slaves to sin" (Romans 6:6).

- "We are those who have died to sin; how can we live in it any longer?" (Romans 6:2)

- "We were therefore buried with him through baptism into death in order that, just as Christ was raised from the dead through the glory of the Father, we too may live a new life" (Romans 6:4).
- "For if we have been united with him in a death like his, we will certainly also be united with him in a resurrection like his" (Romans 6:5).
- "Anyone who has died has been set free from sin" (Romans 6:7).

If we believe the Bible is the word of God (and, surely, we do), then it is impossible to deny that our sinful bodies are dead. As I have mentioned, however, there are legitimate reasons to doubt this biblical truth because, as honest believers, we must admit that we continue to lose many battles with temptation and sin. I have personally found that clarification in the areas of justification, sanctification, and glorification helps people understand how the sinful body can be dead even though they still lose battles with sin sometimes in their personal lives.

First, we must ask ourselves: What do these terms mean, and how do they relate to our understanding and experience of salvation?

The first term, *justification*, pertains to our legal standing before God. When we confess our need of Christ and claim Him by faith as our Savior, this means—not only that we are forgiven—but also that we are accepted by God as He accepts His Son. We are viewed by God as perfect and sinless; therefore, we are regarded as one who does not deserve punishment. The result of justification is that we become a just person in God's sight and are therefore delivered from the *penalty* of sin.

Sanctification pertains to the continual work of the Holy Spirit in our lives to conform us to the image of Christ. This is an ongoing work that enables us to progress toward spiritual maturity and to bear the fruit of the Spirit (Galatians 5:22, 23). Sanctification brings practical holiness into our lives and thus allows us to be set apart for God's service. The result of sanctification is that we are delivered from the *power* of sin.

Glorification pertains to our final deliverance at the second coming of Christ when this mortal nature puts on immortality (1 Corinthians 15:54). It represents the culmination of the salvation process, and it delivers us from the *presence* of sin.

When we properly understand these three terms, we realize that we are delivered from the presence of sin only when we are glorified at the second coming of Christ. For this reason, we should not expect to reach a point of "holy flesh" at any time in this life. That is, we should not expect to reach a point where we are not dealing with the presence of sin in our lives. And the presence of sin in our lives will inevitably bring times of temptation. Times of temptation will unfortunately bring times when we fall under the power of temptation because sanctification is the work—not of a week or two—but, rather, of a lifetime.

Expecting an immediate state of sinlessness after one accepts Jesus as one's Savior is always a sign of spiritual immaturity because each of us has many lessons to learn, and lessons learned in this life are often the result of countless failures over many years. If we have experienced true salvation in Christ, however, we have likewise experienced God speaking tender words of acceptance to us; therefore, we should not become frantic and unsettled when we fall under the power of sin. We should simply seek to learn the lesson of grace that God is seeking to impart to us and then move forward in faith.

Consider the experience of King Solomon. Most would agree that, apart from Christ, King Solomon was the wisest man ever to walk the earth. Yet, Solomon had to be brought to the point where he could see the vanity of life to know firsthand that all striving after pleasure and fame is really a striving after the wind (Ecclesiastes 1, 2). He did not reach this place of enlightened perspective because his father, King David, taught him to keep God's law. On the contrary, he fell deeply into all sorts of sin after hearing his earthly father's instruction. Solomon was brought to the point of seeing the true wisdom of God's ways only after following a path where he said to himself, "Come now, I will make a test of pleasure; enjoy yourself" (Ecclesiastes 2:1). During this time, he withheld no pleasure from himself (Ecclesiastes 2:10). He ultimately found this path of pleasure to be one that led to suffering and pain—and the chastening of God (2 Samuel 7:12–15; 1 Kings 11:9–13).

Do we think the process will be any different for us? What child is there—other than our Savior Himself—who always obeys when he or she is told to do so? Like Solomon, we need to be brought to the point where we see that all manner of sin is merely a vain path of non-fulfillment, and this realization takes time.

There is also the experience of the children of Israel when they were about to enter the Promised Land. (I mentioned this in chapter 8.) You will recall that God said to them, "The Lord your God will clear away these nations before you little by little; you may not make an end of them at once, lest the wild beasts grow too numerous for you" (Deuteronomy 7:22). Since the heathen nations during this time represent the devil's strongholds in our lives, we should not think that we are failing to grow in grace simply because all of Satan's strongholds do not instantly disappear for us at conversion. As I have mentioned, God is growing us in ways that are consistent with His perfect principles of harmony and balance, and we will often learn important lessons of trust through repeated failure.

So, neither the fact that we experience temptations to sin in our lives nor the fact that we sometimes fall under the power of sin in our lives indicates that our sinful bodies are not dead. For this reason, we should not fret during crises in our lives when we are weak in moral power and are therefore prone to fall into various types of sin. We are still God's children during these periods, and our sinful bodies are still dead.

> *The critical factor in determining whether our sinful bodies are dead is this: How do we feel after we have committed sin? Do we feel satisfied and content? Or do we feel remorseful and repentant?*

The critical factor in determining whether our sinful bodies are dead is this: How do we feel *after* we have committed sin? Do we feel satisfied and content? Or do we feel remorseful and repentant? If we feel remorseful and repentant, then this shows that there is no life in our sinful bodies. For if there were life in them, we would by no means feel remorseful and repentant after committing sin; rather, we would feel energized and invigorated. We would always enjoy it, and we would feel stimulated and satisfied after committing it.

A few revealing questions:

- Do you enjoy making life difficult for people?
- Do you enjoy making them stumble and fall?
- Does this activity make you feel good about yourself?

Listen to what God's Word says about those who are in rebellion to Him: "They cannot rest until they do evil; they are robbed of sleep till they make someone stumble" (Proverbs 4:16). God's Word is here stating that those who are in high-handed rebellion to Him (1) enjoy making other people stumble and (2) are robbed of sleep unless they have done this to someone.

Would you be robbed of sleep if you had not made someone stumble? Surely this is not true of you. Rather, you would be robbed of sleep if you *did* make someone stumble.

Are you beginning to see the difference between someone whose body of sin is dead and someone whose body of sin is throbbing with life? Remember, unconverted people of the world *like* sin. They do not feel remorse when they do the sort of things that would make you and me cringe in shame and cry out in repentance. This is the difference between someone whose sinful body is alive and someone whose sinful body is dead.

It is because our sinful bodies are dead that we feel repentant and remorseful when we sin against our Father in heaven. We do not simply feel the conviction of wrongdoing in the way that people of the world do (John 16:8). Rather, we feel genuine sadness and sorrow that we have wounded our Father's heart. We feel this because the new creation in Christ (2 Corinthians 5:17) has replaced the old man of sin (who is now dead) as the sentient power in our lives.

Once we understand that our sinful body is dead, we likewise understand that there is no need to wallow in self-hatred. We realize that the hatred of self of which Christ spoke (Luke 14:26) is hatred of the old man of sin who, admittedly, was in full control before we came to Jesus. But once we come to Him, our sinful bodies are put to death; therefore, any continuing self-hatred is hatred toward God's new creation in Christ—and who would want to hate this? Such hatred accomplishes nothing. On the contrary, it simply hinders us from growing in God's grace.

Understanding this truth that our sinful bodies are dead in Christ provides tremendous empowerment during trying times. It provides this empowerment because it allows us to realize that there is no place for self-hatred in the life, and this realization keeps us from becoming immersed in the many self-destructive lifestyles that are the inevitable result of self-hatred. Self-destructive patterns of behavior will always emerge in the lives of those who hate themselves, for no one can live comfortably with a self that he or she despises. The self-destructive behaviors allow self-hating persons to "stuff" unpleasant feelings and thus cope with themselves. My usual method was to overeat to the extreme, but one could just as easily employ sex, drugs, alcohol—or even religious busyness.

Most probably do not think of religious busyness as a self-destructive lifestyle, and surely it is not, in and of itself, self-destructive in nature. But religious busyness can keep a person in denial as effectively as anything else. We need look only to the religious Pharisees of Christ's day (as I did in a prior chapter) to see how effectively such a life can keep one in the deepest delusion. Any lifestyle that keeps one in delusion is ultimately self-destructive in nature.

There is also the matter of depression. I mentioned previously how I repeatedly berated myself when I bottomed out. I also mentioned how I focused intense anger (and hatred) toward myself because of my perceived boneheadedness. This type of posture toward oneself will always result in some form of depression, and a depressed state of mind makes a difficult situation in life much more difficult.

So, again, it is vitally important to understand that our sinful bodies are dead in Christ; thus, there is no place for self-hatred in our lives. Truly, it is Jesus who now lives in each of us through the agency of the Holy Spirit: "I have been crucified with Christ and I no longer live, but Christ lives in me" (Galatians 2:20). Let us rest in this truth, realizing that we will not be free of sin's presence until we see our Redeemer in glory.

* * *

Praise God from whom all blessings flow.

Chapter 12
We are Perfectly Surrendered in Christ[25]

> *"Very truly I tell you, when you were younger*
> *You dressed yourself and went where you wanted;*
> *But when you are old you will stretch out your hands,*
> *And someone else will dress you*
> *And lead you where you do not want to go."*
>
> *(John 21:18)*

I once believed that my life in Christ would begin with a perfect surrender to God by the complete submission of my rebellious will and the total abandonment of all my personal idols. In short, surrender came down to something I needed to do.

But guess what? I was never able to make this perfect surrender to God. Despite my repeated failures, however, I continued with this same confused, works-oriented thinking in my Christian walk.

Then I reached the point of crisis I mentioned when I bottomed out. During this period, I was extremely depressed. Somehow, God got me through this trying period of about two years, but while I was enduring this ordeal, the one attribute that characterized me in my depressed state was weakness. I was just *so* weak. Because of my weakness, I could do

---

25 Much material in this chapter (as well as in chapters 13 and 14) appears in my book, *Righteousness Inside Out* (Nampa, ID: Pacific Press Pub., 1996).

almost nothing—and I *knew* I could do almost nothing. Therefore, I likewise knew that I could not make or sustain a perfect surrender to God. I was failing repeatedly in this area of my life.

At some point, I took an honest assessment of my condition and concluded that there were two things I could do:

- I could acknowledge truth.
- I could confess my need.

These were the only things I could do, and even though this was very little, it was still something. So, I did the something I could do: I acknowledged the truth of my polluted, wretched condition, and I cried out to God for deliverance in my helplessness.

The result of this acknowledgment and confession was that God revealed to me that all the doing *really is* done in Christ. He revealed that salvation *really is* by grace and that all the work for my salvation *really has* been accomplished for me in the person of His Son. Finally, He revealed that the doing that is done for me in Christ includes this area of perfect surrender.

Truly, all God expects of us is an honest confession of our sin: "Only acknowledge your guilt—you have rebelled against the Lord your God" (Jeremiah 3:13). As I have mentioned previously, this honest confession of sin is the one act that those of the world will not accommodate. They live in an "I'm okay; you're okay" world of denial in which they refuse to acknowledge any need of redemption.

As I continued to pray and search the Word of God about this matter, I began to see how foolish I was for once thinking that I (or anyone) could surrender to God. I found that surrender to God, like everything else in the Christian walk, is by faith. It is something we claim in the perfect life of our Savior.

If we fail to see that this aspect of our salvation is fully accomplished for us in Christ, then we are left in a most precarious condition because we will have little, if any, confidence before God to claim the blessings of the Christian walk. This is so because we will be acutely aware of our lack of total, perfect surrender, so we will believe that we have no legitimate right to claim anything from the pure and holy One. There are few areas where our faith is so severely compromised as right here.

This dilemma will be resolved only when we realize that our surrender to God is something that we simply cannot supply; therefore, we must claim it by faith in Christ. In short, only Jesus lived a life of perfect surrender, and all that you and I can do is simply look to His perfectly surrendered life and then, by grace through faith, claim it as our own before God.

Someone might object, saying: "If we cannot even surrender to God, then what *can* we do? Surely there is something that believers must contribute to their salvation."

I would say that the only "something" we contribute is an honest and desperate cry to the Almighty for deliverance. Listen again to what God says through His prophet Hosea: "They do not cry out to me from their hearts, but wail on their beds" (Hosea 7:14). This is the only real issue in anyone's salvation—crying out to God from an honest heart that is willing to confess its desperate need of Jesus as Savior.

Remember the parable that Christ told about the Pharisee and the tax collector going to the temple to pray? After mentioning the works-oriented prayer of the Pharisee, our Savior stated, "But the tax collector stood at a distance. He would not even look up to heaven, but beat his breast and said, 'God, have mercy on me, a sinner.' I tell you that this man, rather than the other, went home justified before God" (Luke 18:13, 14).

According to Christ Himself, therefore, the simple heart cry of, "God, have mercy on me, a sinner," is all that is necessary for one to be "justified before God." Clearly, a cry for mercy from an honest heart implies that the one crying out will *accept* the offered provision of grace in Christ—that is, he or she will *believe* in Jesus as his or her Savior.

> *According to Christ Himself, therefore, the simple heart cry of, "God, have mercy on me, a sinner," is all that is necessary for one to be "justified before God."*

If one thinks that making this simple heart cry for mercy the sole condition of salvation makes matters easy—well, yes and no. Matters will be easy in the sense that there are no works that God requires from us to be saved because all the works are fully accomplished in Christ. However, matters will not be easy since crying out to the Almighty and admitting that we cannot do anything is the absolute hardest thing for proud, arrogant creatures like ourselves to confess.

If we truly allow ourselves to be broken, to cry out to God and to trust only Him with our whole hearts, then we will find ourselves engaged in the greatest battle of our lives. We will realize how *un*comfortable it is for proud, self-seeking human nature to place its complete trust in a higher power, and we will thus see our need of Christ's victory in this area. As I mentioned in Chapter 2, we would be far more comfortable moaning and groaning and griping and complaining about everything that is wrong with our lives. All our elaborate excuses have become like a nice, soft easy chair or a group of sympathizing friends, and we are quite accustomed to settling into them.

- They are comfortable.
- They keep us protected.
- They allow us to continue in our proud, arrogant ways.

To cry out to God from the depths of our hearts means that we renounce the right to murmur and complain, for, in crying out to the Almighty, we are enlisting the help of One who is both all-knowing and all-loving. We thus have the unfailing assistance of One who is "too wise to err and too good to do us harm."[26]

For the sinless, unfallen angels, depending upon their Creator is the easiest thing to do, but for proud, fallen beings like you and me, it is the hardest. This is so because the peace and harmony that God seeks to impart to us through our dependence upon Him is entirely incompatible with the pride and ambition that is so deeply rooted in our fallen human hearts.

When I was struggling with this issue, I remember asking God to give me a promise from His Word that would help me to rest in the assurance that He had taken this responsibility for my surrender completely upon Himself. Do you know the promise I believe He gave to me? It is one I never would have expected, and it is also one I had never heard used in this context. It is the verse I quoted at the beginning of this chapter: "Very truly I tell you, when you were younger you dressed yourself and went where you wanted; but when you are old you will stretch out your hands,

---

[26] Ellen White, *The Upward Look* (Hagerstown, MD: Review and Herald, 1982), p. 125.

and someone else will dress you and lead you where you do not want to go" (John 21:18).

Jesus spoke these words to Peter to inform him about the type of martyrdom he would eventually undergo. This type of martyrdom was, of course, crucifixion, and Peter is reputed to have been crucified upside down because he felt too unworthy to be tortured in the same manner as his Savior and Lord. In the life of the believer, crucifixion represents the death to self that is indicative of a perfectly surrendered life. Jesus' promise to Peter therefore came to represent Jesus' assurance to me that, as I rest in His life of perfect surrender, I am accepted with all my waywardness, and the Father is fully able to bring me—even *me!*—to a place that my carnal flesh does "not want to go."

To summarize, perfect surrender is something that was accomplished for us in the life of our Savior. Therefore, it is something that God desires that we claim in Christ. We should not look to ourselves or to our personal experiences in this area. Rather, we should steadfastly keep our eyes upon Jesus and keep claiming His life of perfect submission before the Father. We should remain in the mode of crying out to God from our hearts—especially during the difficult times in our lives—for this is surely the mode that allows us to be transparent and authentic before Him. As the psalmist wrote: "Search me, O God, and know my heart; try me, and know my anxieties; and see if there is any wicked way in me, and lead me in the way everlasting" (Psalm 139:23-24 NKJV).

Praise God for perfect surrender in Christ Jesus.

* * *

Praise God from whom all blessings flow.

Chapter 13
We Are Secure in Christ

> *Whoever dwells in the shelter of the Most High*
> *Will rest in the shadow of the Almighty,*
> *I will say of the LORD,*
> *"He is my refuge and my fortress,*
> *My God, in whom I trust."*
>
> *(Psalm 91:1, 2)*

The truth about our security in Christ is a powerful one, and it will bring rapid growth if it is understood and heartily embraced. The point of this truth is that everything that reaches us as believers—and this means everything, even a hard, crunching trial—is divinely ordained by God for our good and must therefore be received as such.

Consider some of the expressions contained in the two short verses of Scripture quoted above: "the shelter of the Most High," "the shadow of the Almighty," "my refuge," and "my fortress." This type of expression is found repeatedly in the Psalms, and it implies in the strongest possible sense that we who abide in the Savior are secure.

Surely, we understand that refuges and fortresses were places of impregnable safety and protection during biblical times. One could not, for example, drop a nuclear bomb on a fortress like Jericho. The residents of Jericho were therefore secure in such a fortress. This is why

God brought down the walls of this city for His people (Joshua 6:20). The obvious point of this biblical metaphor concerning refuges and fortresses is that God's children are secure in Christ, and if we are secure, then we are in a position where nothing reaches us except that which God allows. And that which God allows, He allows for a purpose.

Even though the Bible is clear that God's children are secure in Christ, I think all of us must acknowledge that during times of adversity we often do not feel secure at all. Indeed, we often feel that we are bombarded by people and circumstances that wreak pure havoc upon us, and these times make us feel quite *in*secure. This was happening for me in significant ways when I was bottoming out. I was encountering situations that were extreme hardships, and the personalities involved in these situations were quite challenging for me. The result of these occurrences was that I often felt resentment or even bitterness because the people and circumstances in my life seemed to be hurting me rather than helping me. The thought of being secure in the refuge of a loving and merciful God was often the furthest thought from my mind.

But I *was* secure, nonetheless, in the refuge of a loving and merciful God. The problem was that I was wrestling with flesh and blood instead of seeing the divine purpose in my predicament. I was focusing upon myself as a poor victim; therefore, I failed to see how the behavior I was encountering in others was *my* behavior in former years. My proud and arrogant ways had "gone around" and "come around," and now I was meeting up with them as they were "incarnated" in other people. I was being brought over the same ground that I had caused others to pass, and I was feeling what I had caused others to feel because of my former lack of sympathy and tenderness.

It took me awhile to see God's hand in all this, but He gently led me to a place where I understood that it was His love that had decreed this time in my life (and other like it as well!). I also understood that He was using challenging personalities to help me acknowledge and confess my own hardness of heart. God would bring people into my life whom I did not like at all, and He would keep them in my life until I was finally able to acknowledge, "Yes, Lord, I used to be that way." I would then repent of this behavior and, of course, ask God for His forgiveness. I was learning through this process that even undesirable places are, in fact, protective refuges where only that which God allows reaches us. I was also learning that God uses these undesirable places that appear to be curses, and He turns them into blessings (Deuteronomy 23:5).

Let's consider the experience of Jacob to get a biblical example of this truth.

In chapter 32 of the book of Genesis, we read of Jacob returning to meet his brother, Esau, and he is filled with "great fear and distress" (Genesis 32:7). He fears Esau's wrath because of the way he deceived Esau many years prior. Jacob eventually sends his family ahead of him and remains behind in order to spend the night in prayer. He asks God for deliverance from the hand of Esau, who is now coming to meet him with "four hundred men" (Genesis 32:6).

Once Jacob is left alone, someone begins to wrestle with him (Genesis 32:24). Who could this be? Is it Esau or possibly one of Esau's mighty men? Jacob wrestles for his life, but eventually he realizes that the "assailant" is none other than God Himself, so he seeks and receives God's blessing. Thus, a time that Jacob initially regarded as a life-threatening curse becomes a time of great benefit and favor (Genesis 32:24–32).

God does not normally reveal Himself to us by physically wrestling with us in the night as He did with Jacob. Nevertheless, He *does* reveal Himself to us through the circumstances of our lives. If we understand that we are abiding in a divinely protected refuge where all circumstances must first be allowed by Him, then we put ourselves in the position to receive—not the curse we are dreading—but, rather, the blessing that God Himself has prepared.

It doesn't matter that Satan is the god of this world (2 Corinthians 4:4) and that he initiates most of the activity that reaches us. We are still abiding in God's protected refuge and fortress (Psalm 91:2). Therefore, anything that finds its way to us must first pass through the walls of protection that guard this fortress, and God—not Satan—is the only One who can allow this. The bottom line is this: Any beef we have about the people or circumstances in our lives is ultimately a beef with God and with Him alone. We may think we have a beef with someone else. We may think we have a legitimate gripe about our situation. But we don't. We really don't.

Would any of us complain about the vessel in which some medication is dispensed if the medication tastes bitter? Would it make sense to do this? The real beef is with the physician who prescribed the medication, right? Likewise, our beef is not with any specific person or situation that happens to be in our lives, for these are mere "vessels" that contain the substance that our merciful heavenly Father has deemed best for us. Our real beef is with the Great Physician who prescribed the therapy.

Whenever we are in difficult situations, we need to remember that, ultimately, it is just God and us wrestling on the banks of the river Jabbok as in the time of Jacob. The sooner we understand that it is none other than our heavenly Father who is manifesting Himself in the circumstances of our lives, the sooner we will cease to treat these circumstances as intrusions of the enemy. We will then begin to embrace them as appointments from God.

I do not mean to imply by this that we must simply accept everything in our lives in a passive manner, for God often allows antagonistic people or circumstances into our lives for the very purpose of arousing us to aggressive action. In this way, we become braced to resist further inroads by the enemy. So, again, the fact that we embrace the circumstances of our lives as appointments from God does not mean that we simply accept everything in a passive manner. Yet, the central point still remains: God could have arranged the circumstances of our lives in a hundred different ways to have kept us from crossing paths with certain people or from entering into certain situations. (God transcends time!) The fact that He has allowed our various situations, when He could easily have prevented them, means only one thing: He has allowed the persons or situations to enter our lives for a purpose.

We will doubtless find ourselves thinking that the grass is greener in someone else's life. Such thinking is deeply rooted in us. Nevertheless, we can rest assured that there is a blessing in all the brown patches in our "less than green" lots—just as there was a blessing for Jacob. This does not mean that God intends for us to live with the brown patches in our lots forever, but we can be sure that owning our issues and being open to God's method of honestly taking responsibility for them are all part of our divinely appointed development plan.

We see, for example, that Jacob owned his issues and took responsibility for them. God brought him to a point in his life where he was willing to honestly face his brother after his wrongful deception, and he was also willing to endure any consequences that ensued because of his choices. In short, Jacob did not run from the big brown patch in his life. He did not keep his wrongful deed hidden while stuffing feelings of guilt or shame. Rather, he faced it in the strength that God provided. God then turned the curse of a severed relationship into a great blessing by miraculously restoring that relationship as only God can do. The Bible states that when Esau and his four hundred men reached Jacob, Esau did not attack Jacob. Rather, he "embraced him" and "kissed him," and "they wept" together (Genesis 33:4).

Here is a beautiful passage that punctuates this point about our security in Christ:

> The Father's presence encircled Christ, and nothing befell Him but that which infinite love permitted for the blessing of the world. Here was His source of comfort, and it is for us. He who is imbued with the Spirit of Christ abides in Christ. The blow that is aimed at him falls upon the Saviour, who surrounds him with His presence. Whatever comes to him comes from Christ. He has no need to resist evil, for Christ is his defense. Nothing can touch him except by our Lord's permission, and "all things" that are permitted "work together for good to them that love God."[27]

Once I understood—*really* understood—that I was secure in my Father's care, I was able to see how He was working through unpleasant situations and people to effect a great work of grace in my life. I even began to understand that He could accomplish this work in no other way.

Prior to this understanding, I always thought of unpleasant situations and persons in my life in negative, works-oriented ways. I would think, *Boy, I must really be off track if I have to deal with this person and this situation!* I would then think that I needed to try harder to be a good person to deserve better people and situations in my life, and I would go backward instead of forward. It became a vicious downward spiral. But understanding my security in Christ changed everything for me. I was finally able to rest in my Father's care. I let the full weight and management of any crisis in my life fall fully upon His almighty shoulders—much as I am now letting the full weight of my body fall on the structure of the chair beneath me. I trust the support of the chair, so I can rest. I likewise trust the support of God—even in the hardest times—so, again, I can rest.

Truly, each of us is secure in our Father's care when we come to Christ, regardless of the extremity of the present situation or the apparent hopelessness that we might feel.

* * *

Praise God from whom all blessings flow.

---

[27] Ellen White, *Thoughts from the Mount of Blessing* (https://1ref.us/zc, accessed February 10, 2020), p. 71.

Chapter 14
We Are Reconciled to Our Past in Christ

"Forget the former things,
Do not dwell on the past.
"See, I am doing a new thing!
Now it springs up;
Do you not perceive it?
I am making a way in the wilderness
And streams in the wasteland"

(Isaiah 43:18, 19)

Nothing saps a person's energy and enthusiasm for life more than remorse and regret about the past. This is so because the past, by its very nature, is unalterable: "It is so. It cannot be otherwise."[28]

Because the past is unalterable, remorse and regret about this area of our lives amounts to deep distress about something that cannot be changed. Thus, if we are not *reconciled* to our past, we live with ongoing torment and anguish, and this saps our life energy like nothing else. We find ourselves thinking thoughts like, *If only I had done this and not that, then my life would be better.* These thoughts are unrelenting: *If only I had married this person and not that one, or gone to this school and not that one,*

---
28 Inscription on the Ruins of a 15th Century Cathedral in Amsterdam, Holland.

or taken this job and not that one. Thoughts like these often culminate with something like, *If only I had not been so stupid.*

Truly, we need to be free of this, for this type of mental activity will drain the very life from us, and it will not cease until we are reconciled to our past. Only then will we know the peace and freedom that God wants us to experience in Christ.

A predictable response to rhetoric about being reconciled to one's past would be, "It would be easy to forget about my former mistakes and be at peace with my past if I hadn't done so many stupid things and made so many bad decisions." One might go on to say, "But I've done *so* many stupid things, and I've made *so* many bad decisions. I know God wanted me to make different decisions, but I didn't. So, I'm way off track from where He wants me to be, and I'm stuck with the consequences of the choices I've made, and it's a hard life."

The real issue here is that we believe we are not on the path God originally planned for us. For this reason, we feel deep distress because we think we must be satisfied with less than God's best—and how can anyone ever be reconciled to less than God's best? This issue became so prominent for me when I was going through my first difficult time that I remember saying to God, "If You don't take me back in time so that I can make different decisions, then I'm not going to make it through this." This probably seems like a silly thing to say to God, but I can assure you that I was dead serious when I said it. I even remember the intensity and desperation I felt when I uttered those words in prayer, and I didn't utter them as nicely as I have here. I think I said something like, "If You don't take me back in time, then I'm packing it in."

I was convinced that I had wasted the best opportunities of my life, so I believed that I needed to go back in time to make better decisions, taking advantage of the opportunities that were now lost. Only then would I be delivered from the woeful place in which I found myself. If God would not take me back in time, then I believed I was stuck with a life of unbearable misery and remorse.

I felt so intensely about this issue that I clung to this belief for a long time. I believe that such thinking was the biggest reason my recovery took so long. I was probably borderline psychotic for many months (possibly even a year or more) because I simply *refused* to embrace my actual situation and live in the real world.

I eventually began to see, however, that God could reach me right where I was, and that I could receive from Him not only a livable life but also His best for my life. And I could receive this without going back in time. Truly, we always get God's best when we accept His Son as our Savior because we get what Jesus deserves, not what we deserve.

An important point that will help us to understand why none of us is truly "way off track" is this: Our choices do not spring from a vacuum. Rather, they spring from the beliefs, the desires, the fears, the insecurities, the needs—from everything—in our hearts. If our free choices did not spring from the content of our hearts, then these choices would be completely arbitrary, and we could not then be held accountable for our actions. But our choices are not arbitrary. Therefore, we are justifiably held accountable for our actions. This is so because there are real causes that determine our choices, and these causes are grounded in the content of our hearts. For this reason, none of us is "way off track." On the contrary, we are right where God knew we would be, right where the content of our hearts has led us.

> *Truly, we always get God's best when we accept His Son as our Savior because we get what Jesus deserves, not what we deserve.*

Consider the experience of Peter. Jesus told Peter that he would deny Him. Peter, of course, maintained that he would never deny his Savior and Lord—even if he were brought to the point of death.

Yet, Peter denied Christ.

Why did Peter do this? Why did he deny Christ? Our Savior told Peter about his forthcoming denials—not years or even days before they happened; rather, He told Peter about these denials on the very night they occurred.

Yet, Peter still denied Him.

So, again, why did he do this? Why didn't he simply refuse to deny Christ?

The short answer is this: Peter could have refused to deny Christ only if Peter were not Peter. In other words, Peter could have refused to deny Christ only if he were a different person with different beliefs, different desires, different fears, different insecurities, and so on. Then he could have refused to deny Christ.

But Peter was Peter. So, Peter had the *heart* of Peter. And Christ *knew* the heart of Peter. Thus, He knew the choices and behavior that would spring from Peter's heart.

Peter's choice to deny Christ was not any less free because Christ knew it beforehand. No one compelled Peter to deny Christ. The choice simply emanated from the content of his heart—a heart that Christ knew better than Peter.

It's no different with you and me. We are who we are, and God has known who we are from all eternity. Consider God's words to Jeremiah: "Before I formed you in the womb I knew you" (Jeremiah 1:5). These words are no less true for you and me. Since God has known us from all eternity, He has also known our hearts. Therefore, He has likewise known every act of will that would spring from our hearts. This is just the way it is. The result of this truth is that we are never "off track." We are never in strange places where we must settle for less than God's best. On the contrary, we are right where God knew we would be, right where the heart that He has eternally foreknown has led us.

This area of thought relates closely to the topics of free will and determinism, and it has many implications with respect to salvation. How do I know this? I know this because, as I have mentioned, the path my heart led me resulted in my attaining a Ph.D. in philosophy. I mention this only because I want you to know that I am fully aware of how deeply we could delve into an issue such as this.[29] I simply hope that the basic explanation I have given here is sufficient for you to experience the peace and rest of God, knowing that, in Christ, you can be fully reconciled to your past.

Truly, if anything in your past had been different, then it would not have been *your* past. Rather, it would have been the past of a different person, who had a different heart, and who made different choices based on the motivations lodged in that heart.

But your past is *your* past, so it resulted from the motivations lodged in *your* heart. And God has known your heart from all eternity. Therefore, nothing you did or didn't do has taken Him by surprise, and nothing you did or didn't do can change the very best that He has planned for you in Christ. For this reason, we have no cause for worldly regret or remorse. We are precisely where God knew we would be, so we simply move forward in faith, trusting in His unfailing heart of love and grace.

---

29 I develop this point further in another work where I demonstrate that acts of free will are simply acts that are in harmony with the dictates of reason.

God may convict us of wrongs we have committed, and we might need to confess these wrongs to various people. We might even need to make restitution in some cases. All of this comes with the territory of salvation in Christ. We simply trust God throughout this entire process just as we trust Him in everything else. It is important to know, however, that God is always giving us His best because He is giving us what Christ deserves, not what we deserve.

One final point about regret and remorse in relation to one's past is this: I often hear Christians say something like, "God will forgive our past mistakes, but we must live with the consequences." Whenever I hear something like this, I always think, *What kind of God is that?!* Really, it sounds like the sort of thing people of the world often say: "You made your bed; now you'll have to lie in it." The point of this worldly saying is that people must live with the consequences of their actions. And the further implied point is that those same people will suffer because of whatever bad or ill-advised decisions they have made. Okay, I can accept that. For people of the *world*, I can accept that. But I could never accept that for anyone in Christ.

Think about it: If God, for Jesus' sake, removes the greatest consequence of our sin by giving us eternal life rather than the condemnation that we justly deserve, then why would He consign us to live with other lesser consequences? Personally, I cannot begin to tell you how many consequences of my sin God has either removed from my life completely or miraculously transformed into something beautiful. Do not limit the power or mercy of God over your past, for if you do, your life will almost certainly become a drudgery. Truly, our heavenly Father cherishes every opportunity to transform the bad and the ugly in our lives into things that are wonderful beyond our wildest dreams, for He works *all* things together for good in the lives of those who love Him (Romans 8:28).

God has no reason to make us lie in the beds we have made, and He will not consign us to this. On the contrary, for Jesus' sake, He will deliver us from all the consequences of our bad decisions, and He will allow us to lie in the bed prepared for His Son. As I have stated many times: Grace does not give us what we deserve; rather, it gives us what Jesus deserves.

This is grace.

* * *

Praise God from whom all blessings flow.

Chapter 15

We Have a New Beginning (*Always*) in Christ

> *I have loved you with an everlasting love;*
> *I have drawn you with unfailing kindness.*
> *I will build you up again, and you ... will be rebuilt,*
> *Again you will take up your timbrels*
> *And go out to dance with the joyful.*
>
> *(Jeremiah 31:3, 4)*

The truth of our new beginning in Christ is something Satan works tirelessly to conceal from God's children. He does this because he is the ultimate loser, and he wants nothing more than to have us wallowing in despair as he is. He thus seeks to blind us to this truth so that we will believe our cases are hopeless—especially during the difficult times in our lives. Once we believe our cases are hopeless, Satan knows that he has us secure in his grasp.

It doesn't matter to Satan in the least how he gets us to this place of hopelessness. He will work through lustful temptations to wild living in the world or through sanctimonious temptations to self-righteous living in the church—or anywhere in between. His goal is simply to get us to the end of our rope.

I remember reading an illustration about how Satan tries to blind us to our never-failing hope in Christ. The story is told of the day that Satan was going out of business. (Of course, that will never happen in this life—so it is just an illustration.) He was holding an auction to sell to the other demons all the devices he had used to tempt sinful mortals. Almost every device that went up for bidding was shiny and new, and they apparently had hardly been used by the devil at all. This was true of all his devices except the last one. The last device was a temptation that Satan had found most successful in securing his prey. It was quite worn, and it was obvious to everyone in attendance that it had been put to much successful use. The bidding soared higher and higher as the demons recognized the value and power of this temptation in leading souls to ruin. At one point, a bystander asked what the temptation was.

He was told, "It's the temptation to despair."

You can be sure that all the devil's temptations culminate with the temptation to despair. In other words, all his other temptations are merely the devices he employs to get us to the point that we believe our cases are hopeless. Once he has us believing this, he knows he has us secure in his grasp.

We must understand, therefore, that regardless of how sin-sick, polluted, and desperate we know ourselves to be, God longs to forgive us and to restore us. He longs to give us hope. Furthermore, He is fully able to forgive and to restore us, for He has all power at His command.

There is only one thing we must do: Trust Him.

One might lament, "I could never trust God to deliver me. I have made too much of a mess of my life."

I would reply by saying, "Join the club." All of us end up messing up our lives in one way or another—or possibly in all ways. Yet, God is prepared for this. He was expecting it all along. He did not want it to happen, but there was nothing He could have done to prevent it without imposing His will upon us, and this is something He will never do. If we choose to ignore Him and do not seek His guidance and direction, then He will not force Himself upon us. He lets us walk in the paths of our wayward hearts, and He hopes that, at some point, we will see the futility of trying to find satisfaction and fulfillment apart from Him.

It usually takes a crisis for us to see our need. And why does it take a crisis? Simply because a crisis is what is required to get through to our proud, sinful hearts.

When the crisis point is reached, and we think our lives are over, God is there to say, "I can fix it." This is the important point that each of us must understand: God Himself says,

"I can fix it."

Remember, God knows the end from the beginning, so He is not taken by surprise when our stubborn and arrogant ways lead to a crash. Also, He has every resource at His command. He could bring a hundred different persons, places, or things into our lives right now of which we know nothing, and any one of these could change our lives completely. If God chooses not to do this, then we can rest assured that it is because He knows what is best for us.

You may wonder, how can I be sure that God will fix even *your* life?

Read again the text that I quoted at the beginning of this chapter: "I have loved you with an everlasting love; I have drawn you with unfailing kindness. I will build you up again, and you . . . will be rebuilt. Again you will take up your timbrels and go out to dance with the joyful" (Jeremiah 31:3, 4). I read this passage of Scripture for the first time when my sister wrote it on the front page of a Bible she gave to me for my birthday. She emphasized how this was God's promise to me. I recall saying to myself, "No way."

I could write volumes about how hopeless and depressed I was at the time, but the important point is this: God fulfilled this promise to me despite my unbelief. I see now that He did this in answer to the prayers of many others in my behalf. And guess what? I am praying for you. (I pray for everyone who reads this message.) I also know many others who are praying for you. (I have asked them to pray for those who read this message.) So, I know God will answer our prayers in your behalf in the same way that He answered others' prayers in my behalf. This is how I know that God will fix even *your* life.

> *He will draw you with His unfailing kindness and build you up again (as He did with me), and you will one day find yourself going out to "dance with the joyful".*

I think you realize that God does not need people to pray for you because He Himself loves you. He will fulfill His Word in your life if you simply do not resist His working. He will draw you with His unfailing kindness and build you up again (as He did with me), and you will one day find yourself going out to "dance with the joyful" (as I do—although I once thought that was impossible).

I should probably share a bit of how extremely depressed I was when my sister shared this promise with me since this will give you some perspective on what it meant. I was staying with her and her husband for part of the summer because I was doing some painting work for them and others during the break from the spring and the fall semesters at the University of Connecticut. I was so depressed that I remember taking a plastic cover of a garbage can and leaving some money to cover its cost at one of the homes where I was working. I thought, *I can turn this lid upside down and fill it with dirt and leaves when I get back home. Then I can dig a hole out in the woods and crawl into it. I can then lower this lid upside down over the hole with the dirt and leaves in it, and no one will know I'm down there. Then I can just die.* I even remember going out to the woods with a shovel before I realized how unrealistic my plan was because I did not have the strength to dig a hole in the hard, packed dirt.

I also remember waking up each morning and experiencing wave after wave of despair. I would often feel paralyzed by these waves, and I would hear what I regarded as demons' voices taunting me and telling me what a loser I was. I eventually came to regard such billows of hopeless despair to be "Satan's breath."

I will mention one final incident: I called a sporting goods store and asked if they sold guns. I remember the awkward silence on the other end of the line for a few seconds. Then the person said, "Yes." I suddenly realized what a stupid and revealing question this was because any normal person would ask about a certain type of firearm for a specific purpose, so I just said, "Thanks," and hung up.

So that's where I was. I was a mess. Do you think your predicament is worse than mine was? Possibly it is, but it still doesn't matter because God is the all-powerful and all-merciful One. Therefore, He has all the resources at His command to help you, and He has nothing but love and mercy in His heart to motivate Him to do this. So, He *will* restore you.

Is there still a reason that comes to your mind that causes you to believe that God will not restore you? Before you answer, I will mention that I probably had a hundred reasons why God could not or would not restore me when I was at my lowest. I was as hopeless as a hopeless person can be. Believe me, I was *hopeless*. But when I began to search the Word of God as for hidden treasure, I found something I was looking for—namely, hope. I also found life, the very life of God, and this divine life began to renew all the deadness in my soul and to inspire me with courage and strength. I eventually realized that any "reason" I could give why God could not restore me—well, God had already thought of it beforehand. Furthermore, He had made provision for it.

Had I sinned? No problem–He forgives (1 John 1:9).

Did my heart condemn me? No problem—He is greater than my heart (1 John 3:20).

Had my life become a curse? No problem—He turns curses into blessings (Deuteronomy 23:5).

Had I squandered my best years? No problem—He restores them (Joel 2:25).

Had I wasted my youthful vigor? No problem—He restores this as well (Psalm 103:2–5).

Can you think of any other reason for believing God will not or cannot restore you? If you can, then I assure you that, if you simply search the Word of God for yourself, you will find a promise of your merciful Father in Christ that reveals that your "reason" is not really a reason at all.

The all-important lesson about a new beginning in Christ is this:

- If we believe we have messed up our lives in one way or another (or possibly in *all* ways), then we can choose one of two options, and the choice we make will determine the entire direction and destiny of the rest of our lives.

Our options are these:

1. We can wallow in endless remorse and regret because of all the stupid and boneheaded things we have done in our lives,

or

2. We can trust God.

Do you see that these are the only options?

The issue is no longer that we have messed up our lives because someone has pledged Himself to fix our lives for us—and this someone is none other than . . . *God!*

We Have a New Beginning (Always) in Christ

Therefore, the only issues are these:

- Will we admit that we need help?

    and

- Will we let God help us?

Once again, the issue is not that we have messed up our lives because God Himself has pledged to fix them for us. We must therefore simply trust Him enough to let Him have His way with us without resisting Him.

If we trust God rather than resist Him, then each one of us will have a new life.

A new life!

God will rebuild and restore each of us *completely*, and we will one day find ourselves going out to "dance with the joyful." This may seem impossible to you now, as it once seemed impossible to me, but we must remember that "with God nothing will be impossible" (Luke 1:37, NKJV).

One final point: If we refuse to trust God, and we choose rather to resist His almighty love and power, then we will retain our old, messed-up lives, and we will be destined to wallow in remorse and regret for the rest of our days.

So, what will you do? Will you trust God? This is the issue, friend—this is the *only* issue. We must trust the God who created us. We must let Him fulfill His Word to each of us. In short, we must trust and not resist, or, as many say, we must "let go and let God."

Truly, each of us can have a new life in Christ.

He has done this for me . . . repeatedly!

Trust Him to do it for you.

* * *

Praise God from whom all blessings flow.

Chapter 16
Concluding Thoughts

As I bring this book to a close, I hope you are beginning to understand God's grace toward us in Christ Jesus as well as the empowerment that this grace provides during the crisis times in our lives. I hope you are also beginning to understand the all-encompassing gift that God gives by His grace—namely, acceptance in Christ. Finally, I hope you understand that we never get beyond acceptance in Christ.

I realize that I have stated this truth about acceptance many times, but I don't mind stating it once again because it is the most important point of grace that anyone can learn. Truly, this point of grace will get us through the most brutal times. Our knowledge and experience of God's acceptance during the crisis times, when our deeds are returning upon our own heads and making us feel *un*acceptable, provide all the empowerment we will ever need.

Before I became grounded in this knowledge and experience of God's acceptance, I remember reading a portion of Scripture that helped me immensely, and I would like to share it with you in the concluding chapter of this book. It was the 88th Psalm.

Here are some powerful passages from this psalm:

> I am overwhelmed with troubles
> And my life draws near to death.

> I am counted among those who go down to the pit;
> > I am like one without strength.
>
> I am set apart with the dead,
> Like the slain who lie in the grave,
> Whom you remember no more,
> Who are cut off from your care.
>
> You have put me in the lowest pit,
> In the darkest depths.
>
> Your wrath lies heavily on me;
> You have overwhelmed me with all your waves.
>
> You have taken from me my closest friends
> And have made me repulsive to them.
> I am confined and cannot escape;
> (Psalm 88:3–8)

After reading these verses of the 88th Psalm, I remember thinking, *Boy, that psalmist was having the same experience that I'm now having.* I was reading the psalm in many different versions because the message was so relevant to my situation, and I remember being especially struck by the wording of the King James Version. The last line that I quoted reads as follows: "I am shut up, and I cannot come forth" (Psalm 88:8, KJV).

After reading this translation of the 8th verse, I knew that the psalmist had experienced *precisely* what I was experiencing, for, truly, I was "shut up" and could *not* "come forth." I seemed to be encrusted within a hard shell that was impenetrable, and I often despaired of living because I didn't know how to "get out." I felt isolated and lonely *all* the time. It didn't matter how many people I was with—I was still "shut up." And I was still unable to "come forth."

The reason the psalm helped me so much was that I knew the psalmist felt exactly as I did, yet he did not close the psalm by writing, "I am thus lost, and I will never see Your salvation." Rather, the psalmist wrote, "But I cry to you for help, Lord; in the morning my prayer comes before you" (Psalm 88:13).

I cannot begin to tell you how encouraged I felt after reading this statement of the psalmist. He had written that he was in the "darkest depths" (v. 6). He felt "cut off" from God's care (v. 5). He was "like one without strength" (v. 4), and he felt "repulsive"—even to his closest friends (v. 8).

Yet, he still penned these words of trust and hope.

Prior to reading these words of hope from an inspired writer of God's word, I thought that my experiences of extreme alienation and despair indicated that I had somehow wandered outside the parameters of salvation. I therefore believed that I was eternally lost. It even seemed reasonable to me that I was eternally lost because my experience was one of death and not life. I was, as the psalmist wrote, "like the slain who lie in the grave," whom God remembers "no more" (v. 5).

My thinking changed entirely, however, when I read the trusting, hopeful words of the psalmist, for I could see that he did not resign himself to damnation; rather, he cried to the God of his salvation for help. I knew at this point that there was hope for me, and if there was hope for me, then I knew God would use the extremity in which I found myself, not for evil, but, rather, for good: " 'For I know the plans I have for you,' declares the Lord, 'plans to prosper you and not to harm you, plans to give you hope and a future' " (Jeremiah 29:11).

> *I knew at this point that there was hope for me, and if there was hope for me, then I knew God would use the extremity in which I found myself, not for evil, but, rather, for good.*

I hope you know there is hope for you too, reader. God's plans for you are always to prosper you, never to harm you. Remember, the darker your present predicament, the stronger will be your testimony on the other side of His deliverance, and He *will* deliver you—just as He delivered me. He will comfort you as well.

This study is written in the fervent hope that you will allow yourself to trust your life with the Person whose unfailing love and grace renders Him none other than the "Father of mercies and God of all comfort" (2 Corinthians 1:3, NKJV).

* * *

Praise God from whom all blessings flow.

TEACH Services, Inc.
P U B L I S H I N G

We invite you to view the complete
selection of titles we publish at:
www.TEACHServices.com

We encourage you to write us
with your thoughts about this,
or any other book we publish at:
info@TEACHServices.com

TEACH Services' titles may be purchased in
bulk quantities for educational, fund-raising,
business, or promotional use.
bulksales@TEACHServices.com

Finally, if you are interested in seeing
your own book in print, please contact us at:
publishing@TEACHServices.com
We are happy to review your manuscript at no charge.

www.ingramcontent.com/pod-product-compliance
Lightning Source LLC
Chambersburg PA
CBHW070542170426
43200CB00011B/2524